Self-Help Stories

A therapist's stories to teach, heal and inspire change

J. Macgregor

If you would like to be notified of new releases in the Self-Help Stories series, please sign up to my VIP Readers' Group at my website: www.joannemacgregor.com.

First published in 2018
978-0-9947230-2-4 (print)
978-0-9947230-3-1 (eBook)

CONTENTS

INTRODUCTION

What is the very first story you remember hearing?

Was it a once-upon-a-time fairy-tale, a story told by a grandparent, or perhaps a parable from a religious book? Was it the story of bunny-ears told to teach you how to tie your shoelaces, or maybe a tale you created yourself and acted out with the help of your toys or playmates?

Was there a moral to that story? What made that tale so distinctive for you that you still remember it after all these years?

By comparison, do you remember *anything* else you heard the same day you heard that story way back when, or even from that week or month? No? That's because the human brain isn't hardwired for facts, it's hardwired for story.

The human brain is wired for story.

Stories hook and hold our attention. As a species, we love to tell and hear stories — it's one of the few things that separates us from animals. Since our earliest tribal days, when clans gathered around fires, we've loved to listen to stories, especially those that carry a lesson. We pass on our wisdom across time and borders by weaving it in tales that get told and retold. We capture the best tales in writing — these days in books, print media, and in posts on the internet, but originally on cave walls and in hieroglyphs chipped into the stone of pyramids and temples.

Stories aren't just for children and historians — they're for all of us.

We're addicted to the magic of movie stories and the excitement of tales told in TV programs and computer games. We follow the inspirational legends of athletes and the sordid stories of celebrities, and we love the tales told in songs, poems, jokes and novels. We learn our religious teachings through the parables told in our good books; we visit museums to see the stories told in paintings and captured in sculptures; we're riveted by timeless tales enacted in dance, mime and theater, and we can't resist the social stories told in gossip.

Even at night, we weave our hopes, fears and daily mundanities into dream stories that try to make sense of impulses from within, and information from without.

We're a curious species. We want to know what a story is about, what happens, how it ends, and what it means.

Allegory, parables, metaphors, fairy stories and fables — the way humans learn best is to find the nuggets of wisdom, truth, or inspiration tucked inside an unforgettable story. Good stories activate the sensory perception parts of our brain and stimulate our empathy for others. And, while we're absorbed in a tale that engages our imagination and emotions, our mind sifts through the narrative for the lesson, and is *much* more likely to remember it than it would be to retain a dry fact.

In my working life as a counseling psychologist, English teacher, change management trainer, and fiction author, I've seen over and over again how individuals use stories to make sense of the chaos of experience. The stories we hear shape our brains — they literally change us at the neurological and bio-chemical level — and influence our attitudes and character.

I use stories and metaphors all the time with my clients in my clinical practice, both in normal "talk therapy" as well as in hypnotherapy. I find these tales with a message invaluable in getting across advice and wisdom, and my clients enjoy and appreciate them, too.

In twenty years of doing therapy with clients, I've also learned that people are much more open to listening to stories than to lectures or a logical recounting of facts. They're less inclined to get defensive when life truths are woven into a story about someone or something else, than when I challenge them directly. Individuals, couples and families — everyone *gets it* more easily when it's tucked inside an enjoyable tale.

In this book, I share with you a bouquet of powerful therapeutic stories. Some are true, some allegorical, and some personal. These tales are designed to set you thinking, to help you analyze and assess the way you're currently living your life, to challenge the way you behave, and hopefully to inspire you to make the changes that will help you live a healthier, richer and more fulfilled life.

The contents page provides a brief clue as to what each chapter is about, psychologically speaking. Use this to guide you when selecting which stories you want to read. At the top of each story, there are a couple of questions to stimulate your thinking about the issues that are tackled in the story. You can, if you like, just read the stories, but you'll find that the exercises which follow each tale are designed to help you translate the wisdom of the stories into practical action steps. The Takeaway point at the end of each chapter encapsulates the main lesson of the story.

You can read these stories in any order. I recommend you dip in and out of this book. Find a story that speaks to you, read it mindfully, and — for the best results — take the time to work through the exercises that follow each tale.

Stories are great in and of themselves, but life rewards action, so I encourage you to take the action steps to improve your life.

Don't try to do everything all at once because that rapidly becomes overwhelming, and you wind up achieving very little. There's a good reason why most psychologists see clients for only one hour-long session once a week (or even less often than that). We know our clients need time to assimilate what they have discovered into their existing mental and emotional structures, and to incorporate it into their daily lives.

Slow down, take it one story, one lesson at a time. Try to implement what you learn.

I hope that through these stories you find inspiration, healing and practical help in living a happier, healthier and more meaningful life.

– *Joanne Macgregor* (October 2017)

THE JACKET STORY

Is the world treating you badly? Do people exploit you or take you for granted? Have you tried to make yourself more likeable only to find that you're less respected? This is the story for you!

THE STORY

Imagine that you're window-shopping in a classy, high-end mall. There are jewelry stores, pricey shoe stores, exclusive boutiques, and luggage shops with designer-brand handbags and suitcases in their display windows.

As you're strolling along, you hear your name being called by a soft, beguiling voice. You look around but see no one nearby. Deciding you must have imagined it, you turn to walk on, but at once you hear yourself being summoned again. And to your utter astonishment, you discover that the voice is coming from a beautiful jacket hanging on a display in one of the store windows.

(Now, if you're not the sort of person who would stop, drop and drool at a high-quality, beautiful jacket, then you can make this story about shoes, or a handbag, or the best cellphone ever. It doesn't matter — the lesson is the same. For now, let's go with the jacket.)

You stare at that jacket in the storefront, listening to its tempting call inviting you to come on inside and try it on. Normally, this is not the sort of store you would ever dream of going into — it's a high-end, brand-name store, way too expensive, stocked with the sorts of clothes you never have the occasion to wear, and staffed by snooty assistants with better clothes and hair than you. But today you're feeling braver and bolder than usual and so, on a whim, you enter the store and ask to try on the garment.

And it's ... *beautiful.* Perfect!

You stand in front of the mirror, inspecting and admiring yourself from every angle. And the more you look, the more you like.

It's insta-love.

The jacket is made of fine new wool (or perhaps tweed, or linen, or leather — you decide) with a silk lining, and it's in just the color you've always wanted. It's the most flattering style for your body, the sleeves end at the right point on your wrists, and it's the perfect length. It'll match so many items already in your wardrobe and, what's more, it's a comfortable fit.

It's undeniably fashionable, but in a classically stylish rather than temporarily trendy way, so you *know* you'll get years, perhaps decades, of wear out of this excellent piece. Wearing this jacket makes you look slimmer, stand straighter, and feel like a million bucks. In this jacket, you could take on the world — and win!

You want it badly, but you're almost too scared to check the price tag. If you have to ask, you probably can't afford it, right? Nervously, you turn over the tag, expecting the price to be in the region of $2,000. To your enormous surprise, you see it's marked $20. You squint, perhaps put your glasses on, or step to where the light is better, but it still reads "$20."

Right, honestly now, what's your first thought? What's the first question that pops into your mind?

Maybe you wonder if the price is a misprint, or perhaps it's in a different currency. So, you check with the assistant.

"Is this right? Twenty dollars — twenty US dollars?"

"Yes, that's correct," she says.

What's your next thought? It's a suspicious one, right?

"Is there something the matter with it?" you ask, examining the garment closely.

You're wondering if it's shop-soiled or damaged in some way, whether it's really wool rather than an inferior synthetic fabric. Possibly it's only a cheap knockoff of the quality brand name.

"It's real and in perfect condition," the assistant replies.

"So, what's the catch?"

Because there's got to be a catch, right? If it seems too good to be true, it probably is.

"No catch," she says. "I guess today is just your lucky day."

Right, honestly now, what do you do next?

Do you, A: run to the cashier with the jacket — pausing only to grab ones in navy and tan, too — and pay the asking price for each, delighted with your bargain.

Or, B: take your jacket to the cashier and tell her, "Look, I know you're only asking $20 for this jacket, but I've got to tell you, that's wayyy underpriced. Let me pay you what I think it's *worth*. It's a fine piece of the best quality, probably one of a kind, and I know that I'll get years of joy out of it. Let me pay you the $20 you want for it, plus an extra $2,000.00."

I've told this story to many, many clients over the years, and the answer is invariably A, so if you chose that option, you're in good company. Getting something for a good price doesn't make you a bad or dishonest person; it just makes you a savvy shopper, right?

So, next question: having gotten that $20 jacket home, how do you treat it?

Do you, A: Never go out in the rain or snow wearing it, and take exceptional care never to spill a drop of anything on it. Every time you wear it, you take it off as soon as you get home, brush it down with a hair-roller and fabric brush, wrap it in tissue paper, and hang it in a garment bag with moth-repelling cedar balls in an uncrowded, dedicated corner of your wardrobe. In other words, do you treat it like it cost $2,000?

Or, B: do you start off with good intentions (caring, cleaning, hanging), but really it only cost you twenty bucks, and so gradually you begin flinging it over a chair when you're in a hurry — or maybe even on the floor after a particularly late night out — and you don't panic when you spill a drop of something on it. Do you, in short, treat it like a twenty-dollar garment?

There are a few careful and unusual individuals who tell me they would follow course A, but most people choose option B and, again, that doesn't make them bad people. It's unrealistic to expect someone to care for a cheap item with the same degree of care that they would treat a very expensive one. That's just human nature.

ANALYSIS

Here's the point of this story: *you* are the jacket.

You are this amazing, beautiful, one-of-a-kind person. Your worth is priceless. You are the perfect fit for someone — a friend, a lover, an employer, a child. You can make them stand straighter, feel better, be happier. You will never go out of style, because you're not some passing fashion or cheap imitation — you're the real thing.

---

*You are valuable beyond measure. And **you** set your price in the store of life.*

You are *unique*. Think about that for a moment. You are rarer than the most endangered species on the planet because there only ever was and only ever will be, one of you.

We each set our price in many ways. Sometimes in the obvious way of money — how much you're prepared to work for, to sell your art or your services for — but also in less obvious, and possibly more important, ways.

Do you insist that other people treat you with respect and consideration? Do you require that your feelings be valued, your opinions be considered, and your voice be heard? Do you ensure that your needs, desires and preferences are respected? Do you know and respect your own worth?

Or, do you sell yourself cheaply — bending over backwards to make life easier for others; letting others take you for granted, push you around, disregard or even abuse you? Do you have non-reciprocal relationships — ones where *you* do most of the work, are always the first to apologize, and carry more than your fair share of tasks and responsibilities?

If you're selling yourself short, many people will want to snap up the bargain that is you.

When others get you for a bargain price, they may be tempted to get other bargains, too — you may not be exclusive in their lives, just like you'd buy other colors of the cheap jacket.

And secretly, in the back of their minds, they'll be wondering what's the matter with you that you came so cheaply. Are you damaged, or defective, or fake? Are you really the quality goods they first assumed — because if you were, why wouldn't you value yourself more highly? After all, you know yourself and your own worth better than anyone else on the planet.

What's more, most people who get a partner, friend or employee who's a total bargain start off with good intentions in the relationship, but gradually they begin to take you for granted and treat you with less respect and consideration, especially when you don't speak up for yourself, and when you don't continually assert your price.

Most people have good intentions, but some individuals are on the lookout for a cheap bargain that they can exploit cost-free.

Some people are out-and-out toxic. When they discover a bargain (someone who doesn't know his or her own worth), they think: *doormat.* And they begin wiping their feet on you — exploiting, manipulating, using and abusing.

What's worse, the more you are on the receiving end of this kind of poor treatment, the more negatively you begin to feel about yourself, and the less likely you are to challenge things.

The other person, who always suspected there was something wrong with you anyway, now begins telling you there is. You're so stupid, fat, or ugly. You're oversensitive, imagining things, just plain crazy. You're the worst thing that ever happened to them, you ruined their life or their business, they hate you! After a while, you believe them. You believe that you deserve this treatment, that you aren't worthy of more.

Now if you set a high price on yourself, many people will just walk on by. If you insist on being treated with consideration and respect, if you demand a fair wage, or if you refuse to tolerate poor treatment, many potential friends, lovers and employers will consider that just too expensive, and not "buy" you. And *you want this!*

If they're looking for a bargain-basement deal that they can kick around, disregard, or use as a doormat or punching bag, then you do not want to be in a relationship with them.

Let them go. Give them a friendly wave as they disappear from view.

Those who see your value, and are prepared to "pay" for your full worth in the way they treat you — these are the people you can invite into the store to try you on. When they pay the full price, they are more likely to continue treating you well because they believe you're worth it.

ACTION STEPS

1. Know your worth.

Decide that you are a worthy person. This a decision based on the belief that *you* are unique, and as worthy of love, respect, consideration and good treatment as any other person on the planet. Like all affirmations of faith, it's not based on proof. Don't wait until you *feel* good about yourself, or until you have "proved" or "earned" your worth. Claim your worth — it's your birthright.

Deciding that you are worthy is a statement of faith in yourself. It's a decision based on will, not emotions.

---

2. Display your price tag prominently.

From the get-go, let the people you meet know that you expect them to treat you well. Of course, you need to treat others with consideration and respect, too. I hope that goes without saying.

Say things like:

I would prefer …

I believe …

I feel …

I need …

I think I paid last time.

as often as you say,

What do you think/feel/believe?

What would you like?

Whatever you prefer.

I'll get the tab.

3. Challenge poor treatment as soon as it starts to creep into your relationship.

Protect your boundaries with statements like:

Please don't speak to me like that.

I can work late on the odd occasion, but not every day.

If you ever hit me, this relationship is over.

Let's have a rule that we don't tease each other about our bodies.

No.

Please let me finish what I'm saying, and then I'll listen to your thoughts.

When starting new relationships, start as you mean to go on. If the way you're being treated won't be acceptable if it continues for years, it's not acceptable now.

---

4. Let go of users and abusers.

If there is already someone in your life who treats you badly, then it's decision time. Write down a list of very specific behaviors that you want them to practice (or abstain from) in your relationship. These might be things like:

Don't swear at me or call me derogatory names.

Call if you're going to be late.

Say thank you when I do you a favor.

I require a market-related pay increase every year.

Then use this list as the basis of a discussion with the other person, in which you ask them to change the way they treat you (and listen to their requests for you.)

Give them a reasonable chance to change and if they don't, it means that they can't, or that they won't. Either way, you need to let them go from your life. This may mean ending a friendship, leaving a job, or changing schools. Be sure, when you start again, that you start by setting a high price on your precious self so that you don't merely repeat old patterns.

THE TAKEAWAY

You are unique and precious. And you set your own price in the store of life.

BUFFALO IN THE *BOMA*

Do you allow one bad event to ruin the entire day, one negative aspect about yourself to tarnish your whole self-concept, or nervousness about one thing to spread into anxiety about everything? Then grab this buffalo tale by the tail!

THE STORY

Like many people who live in Africa, I take occasional vacations to one of our many magnificent game reserves. It's wonderful to see how intricately everything in the ecosystem is connected, but sometimes, the ecologists who manage the reserve go out of their way to make sure everything *doesn't* connect. Or at least, doesn't connect too directly or too soon.

Once, while we were out on a game drive in one of these reserves, the game ranger drove us to a *boma* in a distant corner of the park. A *boma* is simply an enclosure for animals. It can be large or small, but its main purpose is to keep those particular animals from wandering off and getting lost, or joining the general population of their species.

This *boma* was enormous and was the temporary home of a small group of African buffalo which had been brought in from another game reserve to be introduced to this park.

While it was a great opportunity to see these impressive, intimidating creatures up close (because it's not usually easy to spot them in the wild), I was puzzled as to why they were being held in the *boma* rather than being allowed to wander freely.

The ranger explained that this was a quarantine zone of sorts, where they could ensure the animals were healthy before releasing them into the greater park ecosystem. New animals could carry diseases and pests to which the local herds had not yet built up an immunity. If just one infected buffalo was allowed into the wider park, the entire species could contract the disease and their population could be decimated.

In turn, the predator and companion species that depended on the buffalo for survival would be negatively impacted, and the vegetation that those animals typically fed on would over-grow, sending the grasslands into a state of imbalance.

They simply could not allow one animal to wreak such havoc, and so newly arrived animals were kept separate until proven healthy. Incidentally, this also gave *them* a chance to adapt to the new territory, and to build up their own immunity, before being turned loose.

ANALYSIS

Negative thoughts, attitudes, occurrences, feelings and behaviors are like new buffalo. They have a right to exist — indeed, we can't prevent them from occurring — but we need to keep them fenced so that they don't contaminate everything.

Ring-fence negativity so that the contagion doesn't spread through all of your life.

Maybe this morning you had a hectic drive into work through the traffic, and it's left you feeling stressed? Unless you make a conscious effort to separate and isolate that stress, it can spread through your whole day, and even affect others when, for example, you snap at an assistant, or are short with a customer, or come home and take it out on your family.

Do you have a pimple on your nose, or have you gained a pound? Stick those perceptions in the *boma* — quick, before you start rating your entire appearance, and then your whole self, as unappealing, unattractive, or disgusting.

Were you trying to eat healthily to lose a few pounds, but you slipped up and ate a slice of cake? Draw a limiting line around that slice so that you stop the behavior from spreading. Don't think: *Oh well, I ate a piece, I may as well eat the rest of the cake, and write off healthy eating for the rest of this day, or even this week.* Do think: *I made a mistake. I'm starting again fresh this minute.*

Are you worried about an upcoming challenge? Watch out — anxiety is a particularly virulent disease. Unless you keep it quarantined, it can generalize and spread to every aspect of your life, leaving you a hostage to future fears.

ACTION STEPS

1. When something bad happens in your life, do you create a generalized belief based on that? It might be something along the lines of:

I'm stupid.
Life is hard.
I'm unlucky.
I'm ugly.

2. Ring-fence that thought as if it were as dangerous as a buffalo with foot-and-mouth disease. A great way to do this is to change your language so that it describes a specific, time-limited event, rather than a general, all-pervasive life rule, or belief about yourself.

Rather than: *I'm stupid.* say *I made a mistake.*
Life is hard. Today was hard.
I'm unlucky. That was unlucky.
I'm ugly. I have a pimple.

Do you see the difference between these two ways of thinking and talking to yourself? The one tears you down with overwhelming and permanent negativity. The other acknowledges the challenge, but doesn't allow it to spread.

Don't allow specific negative experiences to over-generalize into broad beliefs.

---

3. Sometimes, the criticism and insults come from others.

Firstly, remind yourself that their saying it's so doesn't make it any truer than saying the world is flat makes *that* so. Secondly, stick that horrible sucker (the belief, not the person!) into a thought-and-feelings *boma*. Don't let it gallop into the reserve that is you where it can rampage about, spreading damage.

4. If you like, you can walk around the virtual perimeter and examine the species within, and decide how useful or valid that feedback may be.

For example, your partner might complain, "You're always so impatient with the kids!"

Put that comment in quarantine — don't allow it to infect you with a general belief that, "I'm a bad parent."

Now think calmly about the comment. It's only an opinion. Do you think it's accurate? Is there a kernel of truth in it? If so, is it always true of you, or only sometimes? What do you want to do about it?

The great thing about this technique is that it's possible to change specific behaviors or attitudes. If you allow the contagion to spread until you are negative about your whole self, or dissatisfied with the entirety of your life, however, then changing becomes an overwhelmingly big task. So big, that you're unlikely even to begin.

> ## THE TAKEAWAY
>
> Put a strong boundary around those negative events, beliefs and emotions that have the potential to infect and negatively affect your whole self.

FLEAS AND ELEPHANTS

Are you living to your full potential, or do you believe you cannot radically improve things for yourself? Do you feel unsatisfied with your life, but helpless to change it? Read on!

THE STORY

What do fleas and elephants have in common?

The flea is one of the tiniest creatures on planet earth, while the elephant is one of the greatest, but both can be taught to live in very limited ways.

A flea has long hind legs perfectly designed for jumping great distances — vertically up to seven inches (18cm), and horizontally up to thirteen inches (33cm). That's about one-hundred times its own height! Relative to its size, the flea is the second-best jumper on the planet. (The froghopper takes the gold medal.)

There's a classic experiment where scientists put a collection of fleas into a shoebox and measure how high they can jump. Unrestricted, the fleas easily leap right out of the box.

Then the scientists place a glass pane over the top of the shoebox and observe their tiny subjects. After leaping against the glass ceiling several times, the fleas adjust their jumps lower and lower, so that eventually they stop hitting the barrier altogether.

After a while, the glass pane is removed, and jumping height of the fleas is measured again. Incredibly, although the fleas are now able to leap freely, they still continue to jump to just below the height where the glass lid was.

Can they jump higher? Undoubtedly, yes. *Do* they jump higher? No.

They've learned through repeatedly hitting the glass ceiling that it's impossible to jump as high as they are physically able to, and they can no longer jump to their full potential even after the limit has been removed.

Thankfully, the days when elephants were kept as performing animals in circuses seem to be disappearing. In the bad old days, these magnificent and powerful creatures were taught to perform tricks — to stand on their hind legs, or do "handstands" on their front legs, to balance on balls or barrels, or to perform other feats that were unnatural and probably painful movements for them.

To prevent their wandering off between performances, the elephants would be tied outside the circus tent by means of a simple rope connecting a collar on their ankle or around their neck to a small wooden stake stuck in the ground. Sometimes, the elephant could have the rope around its neck not attached to anything at all, and still stand passively still.

As a child, I was amazed by this. Having seen how African elephants in the wild are — scarily powerful, not easily intimidated, and quite capable of crushing or overturning a car — I couldn't understand why the circus elephants didn't turn on their masters. What is a trainer's stick to a creature who can topple trees and trample humans? Why didn't they escape when uprooting the stake would be easy — the equivalent of you or I plucking a toothpick out of the ground?

Later, I realized that these elephants had been raised in captivity. They had been tethered to a metal stake in the ground from the time they were small babies and not easily capable of uprooting it. When a baby elephant strained against the restriction, the ankle-collar or neck ropes would cut into his skin, and he would cease trying to escape his bonds, having learned that the attempt was both futile and painful.

As they grew, the circus elephants were rewarded with food and attention for learning their tricks. They were also punished with beatings from the trainer's stick for their "misbehavior" at a tender age when they were not strong enough to crush their tormentors. Over time, they learned to recognize a much weaker being as their "master".

Now, even though the stake was a small wooden one, and the trainer only a fraction of their size, adult elephants were still limited by their past learning experiences, and they stayed stuck in their current painful reality.

ANALYSIS

What do humans have in common with fleas and elephants?

We, too, can be victims of this phenomenon, known in psychology as *learned helplessness*. We, too, can be enslaved by limiting beliefs.

Bump your head enough times against the limits set by your parents, teachers, or culture, and you'll stop leaping quite so high. Be trained from when you're little that you're not strong, clever, acceptable or equal because you're black, or female, or have some disability, and you may begin to believe it. Be punished, or shamed, or laughed at for striving to be your best, most powerful and exceptional self, and you're likely to settle for being a second-best, toned-down version of yourself.

Even when we are free of those original limiting conditions — when we've left home, we're financially independent, we live in a more accepting environment, when we're strong enough to retaliate against anyone who tries to hurt us — we often don't try. We don't even object, although we may complain helplessly about our lives. We still dumb down, hide our talents and deny our uniqueness. We continue to limit ourselves because of those original harsh conditions and experiences.

---

*The roof and the rope have been internalized, and the
limits are now in your mind.*

ACTION STEPS

1. Identify your rope or roof.

Try to identify what restrictions on your innate abilities were placed on you by your parents, your school, your peers, your religion, your culture, and/or your work environment. What have you been told you *can't* or *shouldn't* do — because of your race, sex, body, age, disabilities, sexual orientation, etc.?

2. Identify why you think change is impossible.

What life experiences of failure have caused you to believe that trying to change will likely be a painful or futile exercise? Think about the times you've banged your head against a metaphorical glass ceiling or brick wall. Based on those experiences, what did you decide about yourself, the world, and your future?

3. What limits do you impose on yourself?

What have you decided you can't do, or have, or become, because you think you're not smart, or thin, or attractive, or talented enough? Notice how you sabotage yourself and dwarf your potential with, *Oh, I could never do that!* or *It's too hard,* or *I can't.*

4. Challenge these beliefs and assumptions.

Ask yourself: Are they true? Are they always true? Identify other people similar to you who have broken the mold, escaped captivity, and broken through that glass ceiling — the paraplegic who climbed Kilimanjaro, the black man who became president, the seventy-year-old who wrote her first book.

If they can do it, then it can be done.
What's stopping you?

Who told you that you were less than, inferior, or unacceptable? Was it your parents or teachers, your sports coach, the bullies at school, or the attitude of the society in which you grew up?

Ask yourself: what if my family, those bullies at school, my society were *wrong*? That's a scary thought, I know. But you know what's even scarier? Living your life within the circumscribed limitations of wrong beliefs! Living your *one* life (as far as we know) in accordance with limits that don't exist!

5. Do a cost-benefit analysis.

Ask yourself whether it's worth keeping the old beliefs, or whether it's simply costing you too much in terms of life satisfaction, joy, health, unexplored potential, and lost opportunities? Make a list of the beliefs and habits you need to challenge because they are no longer helpful or constructive to your life right now.

6. Rewrite your old beliefs.

Craft new beliefs which are more constructive, true or encouraging.

"I can't," becomes *"I choose not to."*
"I couldn't," becomes *"I haven't really tried."*
"I could never," becomes *"I could try."*

"When I'm thinner/richer/older, then I'll…" becomes *"I'll make a start now."*

"Other people won't like it," becomes *"I give myself permission to stop living inside the shoebox of other people's limited expectations of me!"*

These new beliefs may not feel true right now. They may feel unnatural. But the more you stop indoctrinating yourself with the old self-limiting beliefs, the more you tell yourself your new "truths," the more real they will begin to feel, and the more you will be able to push yourself to new heights.

The good news is, you don't need to believe you can before you start trying. Sometimes, we only believe it's possible once we've accomplished it. Just try. *Begin.*

Stop thinking; start acting.

---

7. Identify your secondary gains.

What blocks you from accepting the new beliefs as true? What prevents you from trying to escape your tether?

We do what works. Even when it's self-limiting or self-destructive, there's a payoff.

It's a rule of human nature that people do what works. Take a hard look at yourself and try to figure out the ways in which your old limiting beliefs might be working *for* you even though, of course, they are also working *against* you.

Are they a ready-made excuse not to try something which might be difficult? Do they protect you against the possibilities of failure or rejection? Do they allow you to live in the restricted familiarity of your comfort zones? What are you excused from doing or trying or risking? How does staying stuck bring you some or other kind of reward — perhaps acceptance, or praise for not rocking the boat, or the security of sticking to what is known?

Ask yourself: if you should put yourself out, leap your highest and fail — how would that outcome be any different to what you already have?

If you try, and you fail, how will that be any different to what you already have?

---

8. Give yourself permission.

Give yourself permission to try and, most importantly, give yourself permission to fail. The willingness to fail, and even to make a fool of yourself, is a prerequisite to learning anything new.

When you fail, get back up and try again. Try harder. Try something different. Try until you start succeeding a little, and then build on that success.

"Failures" are only truly useless when you learn nothing from them.

Realize that your failures *are* successes — you've just learned what doesn't work. You've struck something off the list of things to try, and that's taken you forward, even if only by one small step.

THE TAKEAWAY

Get out of the box, pull up the stake, free yourself from outdated, artificial restrictions and limits!
You are more powerful than you know. You are capable of so much more than you have ever imagined.
Begin today!

'I CAN'T SEE YOU

What don't you want to see in your life? What obvious aspect or problem do you unconsciously — or intentionally — blind yourself to? What might it be costing you to live in the dangerous bliss of willful ignorance? This story will open your eyes!

THE STORY

When my children were younger, I used to take them to swimming lessons and sit on benches along one side of the swimming pool with the other mothers and fathers. From there we'd watch our sinking and floundering kids transform, over time, into strong, confident swimmers. The coach's young son — let's call him Kenny — was usually present, too.

Kenny, who must have been about three or four years old at the time, would run up and down beside the pool, splashing through the puddles and wetting the parents. He would constantly interrupt his mother while she was teaching, toss pool noodles into the water, and generally make a nuisance of himself. But he was awfully cute and, as you may have noticed, cute kids (and adults, too!) tend to get away with more than they should.

One day, Kenny was up to some mischief and I gave him *the look*.

Every parent has their own version of *the look* — or they should do. It's a very useful discipline tool! The narrowed eyes, pursed or thinned lips, and perhaps a raised eyebrow, silently but unmistakably convey the message: *you cut that out right now or there are going to be unpleasant*

27

consequences! Normally, of course, we give our own offspring the warning look, but children everywhere understand this non-verbal communication.

Kenny registered my displeasure and stopped his nonsense for a few minutes, but soon temptation beckoned and he was up to his old tricks of disrupting the lesson again. This time, as he passed by the bench where I was sitting, I added a head-shake and a finger-waggle to my look. My silent admonishment worked — he stopped his nonsense, for a little while at least — but that's not the interesting part of this story.

For the rest of the lesson, every time he walked past the parents' bench, he lifted the hand closest to us to shield his eyes. Clearly, he didn't want to see my disapproving mug, but like many children of that age, he also believed that if he couldn't see me, I couldn't see him.

This is why tiny kids playing hide and seek often simply cover their eyes, and then assume they're hidden because *they* can no longer see *you*. Or they might hide behind the drapes with their feet sticking out, or not realize that the bulge in the fabric gives them away.

Young children have not yet fully developed their role-taking capacity — the ability to put themselves in the shoes, behind the eyes, in the position, or the heart or mind of the other. They can't yet fully imagine what other people in the situation will be seeing, feeling or thinking.

So, for Kenny, if he didn't see me, I could no longer keep an eye on him because of that barrier of his hand. As a problem in his life, I had ceased to exist.

His strategy made him even cuter and had all the parents giggling every time he walked past, hand firmly in place.

ANALYSIS

It's easy to laugh at small children who believe that if you don't see something, it ceases to exist, but many adults think in exactly this same way.

Many people think that ignoring a problem makes it go away.

We all develop ways of ignoring our big problems — our growing addictions, our out-of-control spending habits, our miserable jobs, the deterioration of our health or relationships. We immerse ourselves in non-productive time-sucks like mindless television-watching, playing the latest game on our cellphones, or spending hours on Facebook. We work inefficiently, or we schedule our lives full of so many activities that we are always busy.

We keep ourselves "too busy" to deal with our ever-growing problems.

We stay plugged into noise and motion of any and every kind, and make sure we are never truly alone. We avoid stillness and silence, because it's in the still and quiet moments that we get clarity of vision, and we're brought face to face with our problems.

ACTION STEPS

1. Be still.

Carve out an hour or two in which you can be completely alone. Unplug and switch off your phone, your computer, your TV and your radio. Close the door. Sit quietly and just breathe deeply — in through the nose, out through the mouth — for a few minutes. Be fully in the present moment. Gently bring your mind back when it strays off into the future or the past.

2. Take stock.

Do a review of the various areas in your life, including: physical and mental health, family and relationships, friendships, work, spirituality, creativity, and finances.

Check for bad habits — things you're doing (or doing too much of) that you shouldn't be — like eating unhealthily, abusing substances, hanging out with toxic people who bring you down, or being overly critical or negative in your relationships.

Then make a note of things you're not doing (or not doing enough) that you *should* be — like exercising, resting, making time for good friends, maintaining a healthy work-life balance, prioritizing your family, balancing your budget, etc.

3. Make a list of problem areas.

Make a list of everything that you think may be a problem in your life.

4. Make a list of your blinkers.

List the ways in which you blind yourself to your problems and to warnings that things are going off-track.

What do you use as distractions so you don't have to face the scary things?

Blinkers and blinders can be negative behaviors (like anaesthetizing ourselves with drugs, for example), but surprisingly, we can also use benign or even positive behaviors *in excess* to avoid having to recognize and deal with our problems. We can immerse ourselves in a new sport or hobby, work around the clock, or parent so relentlessly that we have no time or energy left over to acknowledge, let alone deal with, our own issues.

5. Imagine a preferred scenario.

How would you rather those problematic areas in your life looked? Set goals (specific, achievable, and with a deadline) for those problem areas.

6. Change.

Start tackling the problems, step by tiny step. Did you read what I said there? *Start!* Just begin somewhere. Take action.

7. Get support.

Improve your chances of success by getting expert help (consulting a physical trainer, a life coach or therapist, a financial planner; or taking a course) if you need to. Make yourself accountable to a supportive friend or group.

You don't have to do it alone. There is no reward, award, or medal for refusing to get help!

---

8. Keep those distractions under control.

Dial down the volume on your distractions. Set regular "management meetings" *with yourself* to check your progress against your goals, to monitor problem areas, and to celebrate and build on your successes.

THE TAKEAWAY

Pretending something doesn't
exist does not make it go away.
Ignoring problems only gives
them time to grow.
Be brave — take your hand away
from your eyes and look your life in
the eye, then do something to
improve it.

SINKING SHIPS

Are you full of heaviness? Do you feel overwhelmed by what's happening in the world? Do you feel like you're sinking in, rather than sailing through, the waters of life? Read on!

THE STORY

How does a ship actually sink? Have you ever thought about it?

We're used to images of ships sinking into water, but the truth is that ships don't sink when they get into water, they sink when water gets into them.

There are a bunch of ways this can happen. All ships take on water when waves (sometimes enormous, rogue ones) wash over their deck, but most of this unwanted water drains from the deck via openings on the side called scuppers. The remaining water makes its way downwards to the bilge.

The bilge is the lowest compartment on the ship, located below the waterline, and a bilge-pump sucks water from the floor of the bilge and pumps it back out into the ocean. If the pump malfunctions and the bilge gets too full of water, the ship will sink.

Another good way to sink a ship is to punch a hole in its side. The hole can be big (from, say, a collision with an iceberg, or being hit by a torpedo), or small (often the result of years of poor maintenance), but once water begins to fill the ship faster than it can be pumped out, the ship's in trouble.

A ship or small boat can also sink if its load isn't properly balanced. This causes the boat to capsize — particularly likely in rough seas — and after that, its progress to the bottom of the ocean or lake can be dramatically rapid.

ANALYSIS

Like never before in history, each of us is immersed in the rough seas of the world, bombarded by its (mostly negative) news, connected to people near and far, and overwhelmed by the sheer volume and immediacy of the waves of information that wash over us. The phenomenon is aptly described by a newly-coined term: "content shock."

Every day we tune in to hear reports of the *big dramas*: wars; refugee crises; divisive elections; droughts, wildfires and famines; Ebola, AIDS, avian flu and the Zika virus; police officers shot and police officers shooting; protests, riots and attempted *coups*; suicide bombings and terrorist attacks; recessions, secessions, economic depressions and tanking currencies; floods at one end of the country, droughts at the other, and hurricanes in the middle; the seemingly unconquerable foes of racism, bigotry, prejudice and intolerance; corporate corruption; horrific crimes; nuclear disasters and oil spills; train derailments and airplane crashes; sexual abuse scandals; global warming, tsunamis, deforestation, and species being hunted and squeezed into extinction.

Phew! I feel overwhelmed just listing them.

And these stories hit us even harder because they are *personalized* like never before. We read the final goodbye tweets of civilians trapped in Aleppo, we learn the names and ages of victims of terror attacks; we scroll through galleries of pictures of the latest natural disaster. We imagine ourselves in those situations.

Like small boats on a stormy ocean, we're battered by wave after wave of bad news. Even if you aren't directly affected, you're vicariously traumatized.

We're left feeling both deeply upset and utterly helpless to change the situation, because ultimately these events are beyond our control. That's a recipe for major stress.

Adding to the big issues, there are waves of *smaller*, more localized news: the death of your favorite celebrity, match-fixing in football and doping in cycling; the latest scuttlebutt about your company's poor finances; the potholed state of the roads in your neighborhood; a new scandal about your president (and mine!); the latest "war" on Twitter, or trolling on social media that affects something or someone you hold dear; news of how our cyber-security and confidential information are under attack by hackers and information agencies — the list is seemingly endless!

And that's not even to mention what's happening to you *personally* — there are cutbacks and layoffs at work; that friend of yours whose life is a constant roller-coaster of drama is having an affair with a married man and keeps asking your advice; your boss is cheating on his taxes and milking his company expense account; you're moving to a new house or emigrating; you've been given notice on your apartment; every night your new neighbors play heavy-metal music until the wee hours of the morning; your kid is sick and your aging parents are increasingly dependent on you; your credit card was cloned and your Facebook account hacked; a hailstorm damaged your car or your computer crashed; you're running up against ever-tighter deadlines from customers, and last night you had a really nasty fight with your partner, friend, or mother-in-law; you're exhausted by the difficulties of raising a special needs child; or maybe today you received a diagnosis of a chronic, perhaps even terminal, disease.

The new stresses pile up on top of the old, and it becomes an increasingly heavy load to bear.

All of these new waves of bad news come on top of the heavy stuff already weighing you down — all that old baggage from your past that you've never really dealt with, but just kept hidden in the cargo hold of yourself: the grief from the loss of a loved one; the scars of your break-ups and divorce; the abuse you suffered in your childhood; the time you were bullied in middle school, or raped in college, or were the victim of a home invasion; or the deep damage done to you by serving in or living through a war.

MAKE IT STOP!

Sometimes, it feels like you can't catch your breath or regain your balance between the bombardments, and you begin to "take on water" faster than you can process it. You begin to feel overwhelmed, like you're sinking, drowning in all that negativity.

Perhaps something big has happened, now or in the past, to punch a hole in your hull. Or maybe it's just the accumulation of a lot of little "leaks" from cracks and holes and broken bits of you that you've neglected for far too long, but it begins to get to you, dragging you down with the sheer weight of it all.

Like a sailor with a broken bilge-pump, if you can't get rid of the stress and negativity fast enough, you'll start sinking — into depression, anxiety, burnout and illness.

If you're already full of the heavy cargo of old traumas and wounds, you'll likely sink even faster. And if the various loads in your life are unbalanced — if, for example, you're working 60-hour weeks, or partying every night — you're likely to capsize.

Overloaded, unbalanced, damaged, tossed on stormy seas — there are many ways for the boat that is you to start sinking.

ACTION STEPS

1. Admit there's a problem.

If you're feeling overwhelmed, acknowledge it. List the areas in which you're at risk of burning out. And acknowledge, too, that you can't get rid of the bilge while more continues to pour in.

2. Schedule a "fast."

For a week, or a few weeks, or even a few months, take a break from what's overwhelming you. Stop reading, watching, or listening to the news (a news-fast); disconnect entirely from social media (a social media fast); or limit the time spent with gossips, and the toxic, negative people in your life.

3. Notice how the world does not grind to a halt.

You'll be amazed at how the world trundles on without you observing and commenting and getting outraged!

You'll find you have more time, and that lots of physical and emotional energy is freed up. Use this to do things which will make you feel better — clear out your garage or basement; read a book; write a book; learn meditation, or how to speak French, or play the guitar; join a pottery class, or volunteer at a soup kitchen. Get fit. Build a jigsaw puzzle with your kids. Write a love letter. Plant a vegetable garden. Bake your own additive-free bread. Teach your child how to ride a bike or drive a car. Have a nap — go on, you deserve it!

---

*Step off the worldwide carousel of craziness and slow
down.*

---

4. Service your bilge-pumps.

What helps you cope better when you've got to deal with the world's
woes? Are you doing enough of that?

For many people, it's exercise, while some swear by meditation or
yoga. Prayer and connection to a spiritual community may work for
you; or spending time with a group of supportive, positive friends,
playing at a hobby, or hugging your pets.

Whatever helps you shed the day, whatever helps you reduce your
stress (without creating more by, for example, abusing substances or
over-spending in "retail-therapy"), do more of that, more regularly.

Stop neglecting your self-maintenance!

---

5. Lighten the load in the cargo hold.

Summon your courage and finally deal with those old wounds
you've kept buried for so long. Get expert help for this. I know it's
hard, and it takes time and energy, but you know what's even harder,
you know what costs you even more time and energy in the long term?
Not dealing with it!

Traumas are big, ship-sinking holes in your hull — you need to get
those suckers seen to.

6. Keep a lookout for the good news!

Stay afloat by filling your buoyancy tanks with whatever brings
light, love, laughter and beauty to your life. You're going to have to

seek these out actively — the news services of the world aren't going to bring the good stuff to your doorstep.

THE TAKEAWAY

Don't take on water — don't let what happens around you get inside you and weigh you down.
Pump the bilge — let go of the bad stuff, as often and as thoroughly as you can.
Find and hang onto whatever floats your boat.

Volume Controls vs On-Off Switches

Are you an all-or-nothing kind of person? How's that working for you?

The Story

I'm not a great fan of one of the founding fathers of psychotherapy — Sigmund Freud. It turns out that he got a lot of things badly wrong, but he got a few important things right. One of them was the idea that we're all a little bit crazy.

Freud worded it differently, of course, but the general idea is that each of us has a subconscious mind (a part of ourselves that we're mostly unaware of), which is prone to being dominated by irrational impulses, forbidden desires and life-limiting fears.

We rely on a variety of defense mechanisms (you've probably heard of some of these — denial, rationalization, sublimation, humor, repression, projection) to help defend us against confronting the unacceptable, scary contents of our subconscious minds.

We pretend, ignore, deny, invent, block out, displace, idealize, and make jokes of some very serious issues in our lives, rather than acknowledging them and dealing with them constructively.

Like I said, crazy.

Before Freud, there was a tendency to think of mental and emotional health in either-or terms — you were either sane or insane, normal or a lunatic. He helped us see that each of us is capable of thinking and acting in truly strange and irrational ways. We're all at least a little bit anxious or depressed or delusional, at least some of the time.

Nobody is perfectly sane. "Normal" is just a statistical concept — the mathematical average of all the variations.

In other words — my words, not Freud's — your psychological health is located somewhere along a continuum, like one of those sliding volume controls, rather than being either healthy *or* dysfunctional, like an on-off switch for crazy.

ANALYSIS

The thing about a volume control is that at either of the extremes (deafeningly loud or inaudibly soft), it becomes impossible to hear properly.

Thinking of things in your life in either-or, black-or-white, all-or-nothing terms is like having the volume turned all the way up, or all the way down. You're likely to be left feeling helpless to change or to live functionally.

For example, if you put pressure on yourself to be a perfect mother, otherwise you view yourself as a useless one, where does that leave you? How are you supposed to fix what's hopelessly bad? And how scary — how impossible! — to have to be perfect all the time.

If the report you must write for work, or the painting you're about to create, has to be *either* perfect *or* it will be awful, you're less likely to begin the project, and seriously unlikely ever to finish, because it will never be good enough.

> *Perfection is the enemy of done.*
> *That's why so many perfectionists are chronic*
> *procrastinators.*

If you're either beautiful or ugly, for or against an issue, fit or unfit, healthy or a physical train-wreck, scary-assertive or a gutless worm, happy or sad, completely successful or a total failure, a good person or a bad one, then guess which camp you're most often going to fall into?

Everything is relative, and functioning at the extremes is, as a general rule, not healthy. Too much of even a *good* thing can be bad — too much water can kill you as surely as none.

We have degrees of health in our different attitudes, emotions, behaviors and relationships, and these move up or down in "volume" depending on our current circumstances, and our relative strengths and weaknesses. I've seen some clients in my practice unravel under conditions of extreme stress, while it seems to get others finally moving in the right direction. I've also seen clients who may be exceptionally strong in one aspect of their lives (in, for example, their careers), be almost unbelievably dysfunctional in another (such as in their personal relationships).

> *Imagine that each area of yourself and your life has a*
> *volume control. It's time to adjust the audio.*

The trick is to focus on selected areas (rather than trying to fix all of your life all at once) and determine whether that aspect is too "loud" or "too soft".

Let's take an easy one as an example. How's your current state of physical fitness? How much time and effort do you put into exercising regularly? Where would the knob point on a one-to-ten volume scale, where ten out of ten is perfect fitness and zero out of ten is a complete lack of fitness? If it's sitting on two or three, that's clearly too low for optimum health.

What number would you like to achieve? A nine or ten? How realistically achievable is that for someone who's been couch-potato-ing for as long as you have? Do you think a goal like that would motivate you, or depress you?

It's likely that if you choose an all-or-nothing goal, your thinking might follow an all-or-nothing pattern, too: *I've tried going to the gym once or twice, but I'll never be as fit as those guys over there — they're tens for sure. It's impossible, so why bother? I may as well give up now.*

What if you were to set your goal to a four or a five — even if just for the short term? It's likely that would seem more achievable and less impossibly difficult, and you'd therefore be more likely to give it a serious go.

Do you remember that I said too much of something — even something good — can be as bad as too little? Too little exercise can be unhealthy, but I've also seen marriages and families fall apart because one person's volume on exercise is simply set "too loud". All that person's time, energy and attention are directed at their sport. They're not there for their partners or children, and even at work their mind may be distracted by thinking about that day's training. Their nutrition revolves entirely around bulking up (or slimming down), and they may resort to unhealthy measures like taking steroids or stimulants. For these folk, it might be a good idea to turn down the volume from an all-in ten, to a more moderate eight.

ACTION STEPS

1. Start noticing when you're thinking and speaking (to yourself or to others) in all-or-nothing ways. Some red flag words that indicate you might be doing this are: *always, never, right, wrong, perfect, terrible, useless, worthless, hopeless, must, have to, cannot.*

2. Consciously stop yourself, and try to rephrase what you were thinking or saying in relative terms, using words such as: *not very, a lot, better, worse, somewhat, improved, less, more, prefer, could.*

Think "louder" and "softer" rather than "full blast" or "not at all".

3. Which aspects of your life or personality would you like to crank up, and which would you like to tone down? Think not only in terms of quantity (more versus less), but also in degrees of quality (better versus worse). For example, more bad sex isn't something to aspire to!

You can apply this method to anything, really, but here are some target areas to stimulate your thinking. Remember — either too much *or* too little can be problematic.

Check your "volume setting" in these areas:

Assertiveness

Friendliness

Social life

Health, fitness, nutrition

Self-esteem, body image

Anxiety

Work productivity

Creativity

Parenting

Sex-life, romance, dating

Managing your finances, saving, budgeting, spending

Communication with your partner, children, colleagues, staff

Political involvement

Philanthropy, charitable work, community involvement

Hobbies, play, fun

Travel, holidays

Rest, work-life balance, downtime

Spiritual or religious life, meditation or mindfulness

Tidiness, neatness of home, office, inbox and digital files

Ambition, goal-setting
Online living, social media engagement, television-watching
Learning (informal or formal study), upskilling, stimulating your mind
Tolerance, acceptance of what is beyond your control
Management of stress and challenges

4. Take action — small steps at first — to start moving that volume dial in the desired direction.

THE TAKEAWAY

The habit of thinking in either-or terms is neither accurate nor useful. Learn to think in sliding scales and along a continuum, and turn your volume up or down where necessary.

TWO KINDS OF PROBLEMS

Do you find yourself carrying more than your fair share of the world's problems? Are you trying, and failing, to fix the problems of others? If so, this story will speak to you.

THE STORY

A long time ago, in the galaxy known as "Psychologist internship," I was one very stressed little bunny.

All the interns in my year were feeling completely overwhelmed by the amount of challenging work that had to be completed if we wanted to qualify as psychologists. We had to complete our theses (mine was on the victim's experience of hijacking), attend lectures and workshops, and complete academic papers. The most daunting of these assignments was "The Paradigm Exercise" — a massive piece of work integrating the various schools of psychology and different approaches to therapy with our own theory of life, the universe, and everything. It not only had to be written up but also presented to a panel of professors, including external examiners, for their critique.

In addition, we had to study for and write exams; conduct therapy with clients in sessions which were regularly observed by peers and supervisors through one-way glass and critiqued afterwards; attend and participate in both individual and group case presentation and supervision sessions; plus we had to do the administrative tasks of running a practice (writing up case notes, invoicing, collecting payments, etc.)

It sounds like a lot, but I've probably forgotten a whole lot more.

Some of the interns were in their early twenties, still living at home, supported by their parents in financial and practical ways. A few of us, however, were more mature students — married, with children to raise and homes of our own to run, which made for the adoption of some serious time management strategies. I'll never forget how one day a colleague brought a cake and bowl of frosting to class so she could decorate a cake for her son's birthday while attending a lecture! Time really was that tight.

My first child was just a toddler, I had quit my job to study full time, and student debt was accumulating by the day. Between the demands of my family and the stress of my deteriorating finances, I simply could not afford to waste even five minutes of time. Each of us felt that we were already overloaded with more work than we could handle, and that we had no capacity for any extra tasks.

The head professor on our course was a talented, intelligent woman who gave you the sense that she could see right through into your core with her shrewd eyes and clever questions. She dressed in brightly-colored clothes and wore bold, striking jewelry, all of which left you feeling a little dazzled. One fine morning, she announced to our class that we were to be given yet *another* assignment, because she needed a grade for her course.

Perhaps we interns were struck speechless by her technicolor apparel that day, or perhaps we simply could not believe that more work had just been dumped into our laps, but we sat, silent as stunned mullets through the remainder of that class.

Afterwards, of course, the grumbling started. How *could* she, we muttered amongst ourselves. How *dared* she? Didn't she understand what we were all going through? She called herself a psychologist — well, psychologists ought to have more empathy and compassion!

We formed a delegation and marched to her office, rehearsing our protests and arguments along the way, bolstering our courage, and feeling rather like revolutionaries on the cusp of a coup by the time we banged on her office door.

She opened the door and, without inviting our little group of nine inside, inquired why we were there.

We can't handle more work, we told her, *we're close to cracking as it is. We've got our theses to do and the paradigm exercise and exams are coming up and all those assignments! Plus, we have a full load of clients, don't forget the clients.* Different interns chipped in with different arguments, all adding to the protest.

Those of us with partners and children added our two-cents worth, too — *we hardly get to see our kids these days, our marriages are taking strain, and how the heck are we supposed to balance the demands of the Masters course, the internship, and our family lives?* I thought we presented excellent arguments for her to cancel, or at least postpone, the assignment.

The professor stood, listening silently, and when our protests finally petered out, she simply said, "My dears, in this world there are two kinds of problems — yours and mine. Let's not confuse the two."

Then she smiled and closed the door on us.

ANALYSIS

I'll leave you to imagine the kind of complaints and uncomplimentary comments which did the rounds amongst us after that! For days, I seethed with anger. I could hardly believe the professor's response. I thought it was unfeeling, arrogant and harsh.

When my outrage calmed, however, a funny thing happened — I realized she was right. There *are* two kinds of problems in life. Her problem was that she needed a grade for us by a certain date, and that was not going to change. Our problem was that we needed to write the assigned paper to earn that grade by the deadline, or our academic performance would be jeopardized. We couldn't remove her problem, and she couldn't solve ours.

In time — and it really did take me a long while to understand this clearly — this experience turned out to be one of the most liberating things that has ever happened in my life. I realized just how many people in the world try to make their problems mine to fix. Plus, I accepted that I was the only person who could solve my own problems.

The world is full of people eager to slide their problems onto your plate.

Many people try to offload their work, their inadequate performance, their underperforming systems onto others in the hope that someone else will pick up the slack, make the issue go away, compensate for their deficiencies, or work around their stupid systems. But those problems are not yours to solve!

Let's take a simple example — one you've probably experienced at some time in your life. Let's imagine that you're a member of a team that must complete a group project for work or school. One of the other members of the team is a slacker who does not carry their weight, complete their segments on time, or even attend project meetings.

How do you typically find yourself responding? Perhaps you pick up more than your fair share of the work, or even complete that person's segment for them. If so, do you get the credit? Probably not. Does the other person get taken to task by a manager and be inspired to make the course-correction needed to avoid the problem cropping up again? Not likely. What they've learned is that you'll cover for them, and you'll likely find this unfair arrangement continues, while you grow an iceberg of resentment in your heart. Perhaps you even try to fix the problems of others so much that you neglect your own work, or other responsibilities.

You may be a fixer in your personal life. Do you try to sort out the problems of your partner, children, other family members, or friends?

Here's an example: you and your friend plan a joint vacation, agreeing upfront to split the costs. The bookings are made, both of you are excited, but then one day she tells you, "I'm sorry but my car broke down and I have to pay for repairs. I can't afford to pay the outstanding balance for the trip."

She looks at you expectantly, in effect handing you her problems on a platter. What is your automatic response?

Do you reply, "Oh dear, how awful for you! How are you going to come up with the money for your share of expenses?" (Effectively handing ownership of her problem back to her.)

Or do you find yourself saying something like, "Don't worry, I'll cover the costs now. Maybe you could pay me back when you're back on your feet?" (Effectively accepting ownership for her problem. Now it's your problem to find that money, and in future, to try and get it back from your friend with all the awkwardness attached to that scenario.)

You may even find that this happens with complete strangers. The cashier in the supermarket cannot make change, so you're stuck with the problem of scratching about, trying to find the exact amount to pay. This is his job, and it's his problem to foresee, and to avoid or fix. I've worked as a cashier, and it's really not that difficult to spot when your cash register is running low on coins and small bills, and to call for change in good time from the supervisor. Problem solved. Customers happy.

But when you, the customer, start rummaging in your purse, you've accepted responsibility for fixing the problem that isn't yours to solve. And the problem *isn't* solved — not beyond this immediate transaction. The cashier now has only a few more coins in the change drawer than before, and will experience the exact same issue with the next customer, and/or perhaps the one after that. The problem continues, with everyone being inconvenienced except the one person within whose power it lies to solve the problem.

Don't misunderstand me — it's a kind and generous thing to help others out from time to time. But you need to make sure you aren't trying to do it *for* them, that you aren't accepting ownership for something that isn't yours to fix.

There's a difference between lending a helping hand,
and taking ownership for someone else's problems.

If this is a pattern with you, if you do it regularly, with lots of people, or if you are in an ongoing relationship with someone (a friend, lover, family member or work colleague) where you find yourself to be the one always stuck with the task of carrying and fixing the problems of another, then you have a problem. And *this* problem is most definitely yours to solve.

For the record, you may think you are improving the lot of that other person you constantly help, but you may not be. Not really, not in the long-term. You may merely be enabling and rewarding their pattern of learned helplessness, and unintentionally keeping them stuck in victim mode.

On the other hand, letting others solve their problems — with assistance, where appropriate — and expecting them to do so, is like a vote of confidence in their abilities. When they tackle their problems, and have some successes dealing with them, their confidence and self-esteem grow.

Our professor had no doubts in our ability to handle *another* assignment. And she was right — we all coped. I could wish she'd stated her opinion in kinder words — "I'm sorry you are all so stressed and overworked, and that this assignment adds to your load. But I'm afraid it is a necessary component of the course. And I have absolute faith in your ability to handle it without cracking up," — but I couldn't fault her logic.

ACTION STEPS

1. Are you a chronic fixer?

Ask yourself these questions: Are you the sort of person who regularly tries to fix problems beyond your control? Do you have a pattern of taking ownership of the problems of others? Do you find yourself surrounded by spongers, lame ducks, and those with a chronic victim mentality?

2. If your answer to the questions in 1 above is, "No," then do a quick check that *you're* not the kind of person who expects *others* to solve your problems, the one who waits until someone else volunteers to help or take ownership for what is rightfully your responsibility. Do you blame others for all your problems and expect some other person or agency to fix them?

If so, cut that nonsense out right now. You can, and should, get help tackling your problems. But you remain responsible for yourself.

We each have our own problems to solve, and you are not excused from the work of dealing with your own.

---

3. If your answer to the questions in 1 above was "Yes," then you need to accept that you have a problem of your own to address.

It may be time to either put up or shut up. In other words, you either need to change *yourself* so that you stop making other people's problems your own, or you need to make peace with the fact that you're a chronic helper, stop complaining about this dynamic in your life, and find ways of doing damage-control so that it impacts less negatively on your own quality of life, time, energy and resources.

4. Acknowledge that there's a payoff for always being the helper and the rescuer.

Your payoff might be that those you help praise you and are appreciative, although, strangely, they're often remarkably ungrateful. (I think this is because, deep down, they feel resentful at always feeling like a helpless victim.) Other people might praise you for your selflessness, or you might secretly enjoy playing the martyr. Sometimes, helping others puts you in a position of power or control over them.

Whatever the payoff, when you admit that your behavior may not be quite as noble as you think it is, it might be easier for you to change your pattern.

5. If you want to change, then when you are faced with a problem that needs to be fixed, stop and think first, before jumping in to take ownership.

Ask yourself:

Is this my problem to solve, or is it rightfully the other person's responsibility?

Can I solve this problem, or is it beyond my control?

Will I truly be resolving the issue, or only providing a temporary quick-fix which delays dealing with the real issue?

If I do what I'm tempted to do in this situation, will that help the other person change their patterns in the long-term, or am I only facilitating and enabling their dysfunctional patterns?

6. If you decide that this problem is not yours to solve, refuse to take ownership for it.

Saying no is not an act of aggression towards the other person, it's simply denying a request.

Pause, take a deep breath and *think* the tough thought, "My dear, in this world there are two kinds of problems, yours and mine. Let's not confuse the two."

You might not want to say it in this way, however, as although it's not technically rude or aggressive (you're not shouting, manhandling, stigmatizing, swearing, insulting, or calling the other person derogatory names, etc.), it does still *sound* harsh and unsympathetic.

I suggest using this kinder phrase: *I'm sorry you have that problem.*

(This puts the problem ball back in their court.)

Then immediately follow up with a statement that shows you expect them to solve their own issue. Try:

What do you think you can do about this?

Well, I'll leave you to figure that one out.

It sounds like you have some thinking to do. Let me know what you decide.

7. Do not rush to fill the silence or the vacuum of action.

Don't feel guilty and don't allow yourself to be guilt-tripped, or emotionally blackmailed. Don't be intimidated if the other person reacts with disapproval or anger. It won't kill you if someone is grumpy with you.

8. Let the other person come up with their own possible solutions or strategies.

You can, after they've had a crack at it, suggest ideas or potential solutions, but you can't do it *for* them. This is tough-love, and in the long run, you'll be doing much more to help that person learn to deal with their own problems and grow in confidence.

THE TAKEAWAY

You can help others, but you can't solve other people's problems for them.

Think: There are two kinds of problems — yours and mine. Let's not confuse the two.

Say: I'm sorry you have that problem.

A GLASS OF WATER

What is your go-to emotion? What tends to be your automatic reaction to life's challenges? This quick anecdote carries one of my favorite and most powerful lessons.

THE STORY

I was once sitting in church when the minister did a superb demonstration.

"Watch carefully," the minister told the congregation, as he poured water into a glass until it was full right up to the brim.

We watched, mystified, as he walked up the aisle and got someone to gently jostle him. Of course, water sloshed over the side of the glass.

"What you're full of, is what spills over when you're bumped," he told us all. "What are you full of?"

ANALYSIS

How do you tend to react when someone cuts you off in traffic, when your little kid drops and breaks a plate, when your partner comes home late without calling to let you know, when your boss adds an extra task to your load, when a friend cancels a lunch date, when you aren't asked out on a second date, or when someone disagrees with you on your favorite social media platform?

Do you get angry, and maybe lash out in temper?
Who does that guy think he is?
What gives her the right to treat me like this?
I'll show them! It's just not fair!

Or do you feel sad and want to cry?
People just don't like me.
I can't cope. It's too hard.

Maybe you sigh and have yourself a little pity-party?
Murphy's Law! Just my luck. Other people don't struggle like this.

Do you reach for a drink or a doughnut or a cigarette to help you deal?
After that scare, day, disappointment, irritation, I need/deserve this!

Does your anxiety spike into a wave of worrying what-ifs?
What if that driver had crashed into me, and I couldn't afford to pay for repairs, and I was left without transport?
What if my husband's late because he had an accident?
What if I can't keep up at work and they let me go?
What if I really am undatable, unlikeable, a failure?

Or do you laugh it off, perhaps accept what you can't change, and maybe even see what you could learn from a situation?
You're having a smashing time! Well, that plate's broken. Let's just sweep it up carefully so no one steps on a piece and cuts their foot. How about next time when you carry a plate you use both hands to hang on tight?

Do you perhaps express gratitude?
Thank goodness that driver didn't hit me.
Isn't it great that my boss trusts me enough to give me this new responsibility?

Well, if that hottie doesn't fancy me, better I know sooner rather than later when my heart would be at risk of being broken.

Anger, sadness, self-pity, anxiety, humor, gratitude — whatever spills over when life gives you a bump, that's what you're full of, for better or worse.

ACTION STEPS

1. Identify what you're full of.

Sometimes this is easy — you will have answered the question above as soon as you read it. Sometimes you may need to think about it, and observe how you tend to react to stresses and challenges in your life. Perhaps you could tell a trusted friend this little story and ask them what they think you might be full of.

Now ask yourself if you *want* this emotion, attitude or reaction pattern to be your automatic response.

2. If not, you need to empty your glass a little.

You need to turn down the volume on this emotion or characteristic, and there are many ways of doing this. There's no comprehensive list of things that will work for every person and every emotion, but here are some to kick-start your thoughts.

- Journal:

Spend half an hour writing down what makes you angry, sad, or afraid (or whatever you're full of). Do this for several days in a row.

Allow your mind to go back into the past, even as far back as your childhood, and note what *used to* cause you to feel this emotion.

Write down all the events and people that make (or ever made) you feel this emotion. Do an emotional "vomit" onto the pages without censoring yourself. If you're worried that someone might find and read your page, and be hurt by them, simply destroy the pages as soon as you've written them.

The goal is to get the negativity out, not to hang onto it.

- Un-mailed letter:

Write an *un-mailed* letter to the person/s, organizations or communities you believe have wounded or wronged you.

Again, this is an "emotional vomit" of the toxic words and feelings you've been storing inside. This letter will never be mailed, so you are free to write what and how you like without fear of hurting others or igniting a feud. You can even write to someone who has passed away, or to something historical or abstract without an individual identity (to slavery or sexism, for example, or to war, greed, or cancer.)

When you're done, burn the letter and scatter the ashes, or shred it and flush it down the toilet, or let it go in a way that feels good to you. Imagine that you are releasing the bad stuff right along with it.

- Breathe:

If you're angry or anxious, make a habit of practicing deep breathing — the easiest is 4x4 breathing: breathe in through your nose for a count of four, hold for four, breathe out slowly through your mouth for four, hold for four. Gradually increase the length of the out-breath. Feel your stress levels and blood pressure drop!

Any exercise which targets breathing, such as yoga, is also helpful.

- Meditate and /or visualize:

Sit somewhere comfortable, close your eyes, consciously relax your body, and breathe deeply.

Imagine breathing *in* peace, calm, and healing. Give it a color as you imagine inhaling it and letting it fill you. Breathe *out* anger, resentment, fear, or whatever you're struggling with. Give that toxic stuff a color and visualize it leaving your body.

Visualize the person who has wronged you. Imagine yourself saying words of forgiveness to them. In your mind's eye, shower them with light, and see them receiving all kinds of good things. (When you wish bad things on a person, it doesn't actually affect them at all. It's *you* who stores the accompanying bad feeling in your body – do you really want that?)

Holding onto rage and resentment at another is like holding a burning coal in your hand and expecting it to burn the other person.

Imagine yourself in stressful situations, but responding in a healthier way — with humor, or tolerance, or gratitude. Mentally rehearse, as top athletes do, yourself reacting in these more constructive ways.

- Practice extreme gratitude:

There's nothing as powerful as gratitude for clearing out negative thoughts and emotions!

Practicing gratitude is especially useful if you're full of self-pity or a strong sense that life is unfair towards you.

Keep a gratitude journal where every day you list three things for which you're grateful. These can be big things (health, life, a job) or small (a great parking spot on a busy shopping day, seeing a butterfly on a flower, a joke that made you laugh.)

On especially bad days, sit down and make a list of everything you're grateful for. Notice that this is actually a list of how life is unfair – *in your favor!* These are the ways in which you're *luckier* than so many other people. (Do you have two legs, your vision, enough to eat today, fresh running water, a roof over your head? Winning!)

For a real challenge, try to find something you're grateful for in even the hard aspects or experiences of your life. Let me be clear: I am *not* saying that bad things "happen for a good reason." I am saying that sometimes — often only a long while afterward — we can harvest some lesson or positive aspect, even if it's only, "I survived. I am a survivor."

- Affirmations:

Craft a statement that affirms what you *would* like to be filled with, for example, *I am a happy and grateful person; I react calmly to life's challenges; I am strong, talented and creative; I stay positive even when things are negative.* Repeat your affirmation to yourself by saying, singing or writing it out seventy-five times a day.

An affirmation is simply a positive statement of the condition you would like to bring about.

You don't have to believe the statement initially, and it doesn't matter if repeating it feels unnatural or awkward. Just do it.

Make sure the affirmation is phrased in the first person (*I* am calm), present tense (I *am* strong) and in the positive (*I accept what I can't change* rather than *I don't try to change things which are beyond my control.*)

Try to keep your statements short and sweet, and use simple words — your subconscious mind (which you are trying to reprogram with this exercise) likes that kind of language.

If you're anxious, practice bringing yourself back from the what-if future to the present. Make this your mantra: *Right now I'm safe and all is well.*

Breathe! Breathe out!

If you're angry, try saying: *Right now, I'm calm. All is well.*

If you're sad, try: *It's okay to feel sadness and it's okay to release sadness. Right now, I breathe out sadness, and focus on the happy moments in my life.*

Done right and regularly, this practice begins to alter your thinking and your emotions at a neuro-chemical level.

- Disprove your reality:

Do the thing that disproves what you're full of.

For example, if you're full of fears of poverty, donate to a cause you care about. This proves you have more money than you need.

If you're full of woe-is-me, volunteer for an organization that helps others who are substantially worse off than you. You will experience the reality of your own good fortune.

If you're sad, set yourself up for a laugh — watch a funny movie or a gag-reel of your favorite TV program, go to a comedy show, watch YouTube videos of babies tasting lemons for the first time. When you laugh, or even just crack a smile, catch that moment of joy and affirm: *Right now I'm happy. In this moment, I am a happy person.*

- Substitution:

Replace your go-to reaction with healthier ways of achieving the same result.

Rather than cursing the person who cuts you off in traffic, mutter (or yell), "Bless you!" or "You have a great day!"

Replace that frustrated groan, sigh or exclamation with something that will make you feel better. I try to remember to say, "I am as the hollow reed — troubles pass through me as the wind," which is so silly it always makes me laugh, and breaks my irritated mood.

Instead of dealing with stress negatively — by overeating, smoking, abusing substances, or venting your spleen on those around you — go for a walk with your dogs, work out your rage on a boxing-bag at the gym, fill a bird-feeder with seed and sit where you can watch the avian banquet, or give yourself the calming treat of a long, candle-lit foam bath.

3. Remember that the way you normally or automatically respond is just a habit.

It's *become* automatic with endless repetitions over time. But habits can be changed! It's hard to eliminate them, but it's much easier to *replace* them with new habits that support you in creating a happier, healthier self.

> ## THE TAKEAWAY
>
> What spills over when you're bumped
> — that's what you're full of.
> Wouldn't you rather be full of the
> good stuff?

THE TENDER TOOTH

What from your past still hurts, and still impacts your present? What are your hot-button issues? Here's a quick metaphor for you.

THE STORY

Many of us will have had this experience. You visit the dentist for a checkup, or perhaps because you've been having toothache, or sensitivity to hot or cold foods. The dentist gets you to lie back and open your mouth, then she does an examination — first looking and then, with one of her instruments, she gently taps each tooth in turn.

All goes well until she hits that one tooth. You yelp in pain and almost leap out of the chair.

"Aha," she says, "that one has a problem root!"

If the root isn't healthy, you're going to feel pain, and function will be impaired.

ANALYSIS

There's a reason why psychologists ask clients about their past, their childhoods, their earliest memories, and the negative experiences of their youth. It's because what causes you pain and difficulty in the present frequently has its roots in the past.

What you're sensitive to, what makes you instantly furious, upset, or afraid is often *not* about (or not *all* about) what is happening *now*. This is particularly true when your emotional reaction is out of all proportion to the triggering event. That's usually a tip-off that you're experiencing transference from the past — that you are *transferring* the thoughts and emotions related to some difficult person or experience from your past, into this present moment.

Your overreactions to your current problems have their roots in the past.

So, what sets you off? Is it injustice, unkindness, bullying, abuse, favoritism, incompetence, or something else? Here are some questions to help you identify your hot-button issues.

What news stories, or scenes from movies or TV programs make you feel truly upset or panicky?

Do you "lose it" when someone criticizes or teases you, especially about one particular aspect of yourself?

Conflict might be your trigger — if there's disagreement in the family or friendship circle, does that make you seriously upset, perhaps even set your heart racing, or make you feel nauseated?

When people speak with passion or intensity, do you find yourself telling them, "Stop shouting!" — even though they're not?

Do you feel crushed — what the Brits call "gutted" — when someone in authority expresses (even mild) disapproval of your performance?

Maybe you can't stand being left alone, or excluded from social gatherings, or ignored by loved ones.

Do you take it way too seriously when you don't win?

Is there a nickname, or a family anecdote, or a childhood photograph of you that brings up strong negative feelings in you?

Does your spouse, or your enemy, know exactly what to say to really get under your skin?

Do you lash out at your children — verbally and possibly even physically — when they behave in certain ways?

These are your trigger points. These are the tender "teeth" in your life, with roots reaching deep back into the past.

If you react with strong, negative emotions to something, then that something usually has its origin in your past — whether that be as recent as last week, or as far back as in your childhood. That's when you first felt the negative emotion in response to something you experienced. The encounter/s sensitized you to the issue, and to this day you still dread it (consciously or subconsciously), and you usually over-react when you come face-to-face with it (or something or someone that resembles it) again.

You may react so strongly that you lash out at the offender with a blast of anger and abuse, an outpouring of accusations and guilt, and perhaps even aggression or violence. Or you might subside in a torrent of tears, "go fetal" (curl up in scary silence or with raging screams), or fall back on negative coping behaviors — eating your way through the contents of your fridge, running away, going on a bender, picking a fight, breaking things, harming yourself, or hitting something or someone.

Afterwards, you may wonder at the strength and extent of your reaction — *Where did that come from? Am I crazy? Why did I flip out like that?* You may find yourself needing to apologize to those you vented at. Maybe those people tell you that you need to get help.

Maybe they're right.

ACTION STEPS

1. Identify the damaged roots.

Start observing yourself. Notice what presses your buttons. Try to identify the sort of situation that sets you off.

Often the easiest way to do this is to recognize when your emotional and/or behavioral reaction is out of all proportion to the size of the offense, and to note when you are experiencing super strong negative feelings. Then "rewind" through the preceding events, and try to figure out what it was that upset you.

Now do the extended visualization exercise which follows.

2. Visualization

2.1 Body work

When you've had one of these over-reactions, use it to gain a little wisdom by tapping into your body's experience of the emotion that you felt so strongly.

We store our personal history in our bodies.

When you have a good half hour to be calm and private, lie down or sit comfortably, and be quiet for a moment. Close your eyes and take a few deep, slow breaths to relax yourself. Breathe in through your nose, and breathe out — slowly, slowly — through your mouth.

Now allow yourself to feel that strong emotion again, and use the questions below to stimulate your thinking. I know they may seem a little odd, but just go along with the exercise, okay? There are no right or wrong answers — whatever pops into your mind or body is just fine.

Where in your body do you feel the emotion — your throat, chest, stomach, hands, behind your eyes, or somewhere else?

If this feeling had a color, what color would it be?

Does it have a temperature — is it hot or cold?

Does it have a texture or sensation — light and airy, thick and sludgy, sticky, prickly, tight, heavy, solid?

Does it move in any way, shifting position or pulsing, throbbing, shrinking, expanding?

Does this feeling have a name — anger, sadness, fear, grief, loneliness, insecurity, rage, guilt, shame, embarrassment, worry, loss, despair, or something else?

Put your inner ear up close to it and listen. What is it "saying" to you? What does it whisper or shout? Does it have a message for you?

2.2 Do some personal archeology

Once you've completely familiarized yourself with this feeling, allow your mind to go back to the very first time you felt this emotion.

How old were you when you first felt this way? Don't try to remember as a mental exercise in recollection, just allow your body to carry you back in time. Notice what comes up — a number, a memory, an image, a word, or perhaps someone's name.

Now allow yourself to remember — it might be a specific event or moment in time, or it might be a general theme from your childhood, or a time period of days, months or years, or just the way things were back then.

2.3 Contextualize

If the experience happened in your childhood, allow yourself to understand that your reaction to what happened back then was normal and understandable. Make an effort to grasp just how *young* you were, how little experience of the world you had, how few resources and skills you possessed to deal with situations or people like that.

Forgive yourself for behaving like a child, because you *were* just a child. Forgive yourself as often as you need to — it can take time to update our story of the past.

Children who experience abuse or trauma often feel old beyond their years, and judge themselves harshly for not coping better, or fixing the situation. As adults, they continue to feel that same way about themselves, even though they would never judge another child in that way. It's an unfair double-standard.

You've got to realize — deep in your gut, not just in your logical mind — how very young and helpless you were.
And then cut yourself the same slack you would cut another child in those circumstances.

If the experience happened later in your life, try to understand that you were doing the best you knew how back then. Forgive yourself for not being able to see around corners.

2.4 Let go of what you no longer need

Focus again on that old, negative emotion — the one that was only natural back then but has outlived its usefulness in the present. Do you still want to lug it around, day in and day out?

I know all that old baggage is fascinating. You can still set it down, and walk away.

If you think it's time to let it go, then imagine sending that emotion, wherever it sits in your body, light and love and reassurance. Speak to yourself in an encouraging way:

I'm alive, I'm okay.
I'm a powerful adult now, no longer a helpless child.
Now that I know better, I can do better.
I can protect myself in stronger, healthier ways.

As you bathe that emotion in light, you might notice that it cools, shrinks, fades or dissipates in some way.

2.5 Ground yourself in the here and now

Take a few deep breaths, open your eyes, and come back to the present. You are no longer a child. It is no longer that time in your past.

Now you need to decide what you're going to do about what you've learned. Is there someone you need to confront, or forgive, or apologize to? Would it help to journal what you've discovered?

It can be very useful to write that person (or time in your life, or event or injustice) an un-mailed letter in which you express — uncensored — all your thoughts and feelings, and then burn that letter and scatter the ashes of the past to the winds of now.

Do you need to learn new skills to deal with that trigger issue — perhaps via a book, a course, or a coach of some kind?

Did you discover something traumatic? Then you will benefit from professional help.

There really is no good reason to still be carrying this around with you. Why not deal with it once and for all? (I know the thought of that may seem scary, but dealing with it thoroughly will take less energy and cause less pain in the long run — rather like yanking out a loose or rotten tooth with one quick, firm tug hurts less than fiddling with it constantly and trying to ignore the pain.)

3. Know your issues.

At the very least, you need to be aware of your "tender teeth," so you realize when you're encountering a triggering situation or person. This will help you to control your reaction so that it stays appropriate and proportionate.

It's not fair to react to this person in the present with all the weight, force and impetus of difficult events in your past. You may like to share what you've learned about your tender issues with your partner, close friends, or family members — those whom you can trust to handle the insight compassionately and maturely. Knowing in what areas you are particularly thin-skinned can help them tread more carefully and sensitively when it comes to those issues.

THE TAKEAWAY

Find your own "tender teeth" and deal with the past so that it doesn't contaminate the present or spoil the future.

DANDELIONS IN THE SIDEWALK

Does the world seem like a grim place to you? Are you getting increasingly cynical, pessimistic and negative? Here's a quick story for you.

THE STORY

When I was doing my internship as a psychologist, I rapidly reached a point where I was shell-shocked by the horror and pain I heard on a daily basis from my clients. There is a lot of sadness, grief and trauma in the world, and I rapidly felt overwhelmed by hearing about it from client after client. (Nobody comes to see a therapist because they're feeling happy!)

Mind you, we intern psychologists still had a light therapy load back then — we weren't seeing nearly the number of clients we would after we qualified — but we weren't yet "therapeutically fit". We didn't have enough in the way of boundaries and resilience to cope with all the accounts of trauma flowing into our ears. The toxic effect was beginning to accumulate.

I had never realized how much pain was in the world, just how many people had been abused in childhood, how horrifically individuals could treat each other, what people had done and had experienced in the name of one cause or another. It began to feel like there was no good in the world. I had stared down into the abyss of humanity's darkness, and was battling to raise my head again.

It's very, *very* difficult to go home after a day like that and respond enthusiastically when your little kid shows you the picture he drew at Kindergarten that day, or to encourage your husband in his career, or to feel sympathetic when friends tell you of the little slights and hiccups they've experienced in the past week. The ups and downs of everyday life pale into insignificance when compared to the horrors you've heard in the practice that day. And that's not right – it's not fair to your family and friends, and it's not fair to you.

One day, one of our professors took a good look at our small class of sad, grim-faced, haggard-looking intern psychologists, and kicked off the day's tutorial with an exercise aimed at getting us focused on the positives in life. Yes, she assured us, there *were* still good things in the world; we'd just stopped noticing them.

"What makes you happy? What gives you hope? How do you recharge your batteries? What always lifts your spirit?" she asked us.

We went around the class (I think there were only nine of us left by that point) and each took a turn sharing what helped them when they were feeling really down. It was different for each of us. Some spoke of how listening to music lifted their spirits, others of how playing with children or pets worked for them. For me, it was escaping into a good novel.

"Those are good," said the professor, "but I'd like you to find examples, not just of distraction or escape or mere pleasantness, but instances of where good triumphs, examples of the goodness of humankind."

She urged us to actively *search out* evidence of kindness, generosity, strength and courage.

We came up with new examples: a mass choir singing the Hallelujah Chorus; organizations such as Medicine Sans Frontiers or the Red Cross; Mother Theresa; Van Gogh's paintings; the nameless volunteers who help out in hospitals, nursing homes and hospices; personal stories of people who'd gone out on a limb to help us; and even the self-same clients whose stories horrified and vicariously traumatized us. Because if ever there were examples of strength and courage, they were to be found in the form of our clients who were still standing, still fighting to live and be happier and healthier in a world that had dealt with them harshly.

The professor also told us a couple of the things that buoyed *her* up, and I still distinctly remember one of those. On her daily walk from the parking lot to her office in the university building, she passed a crack in the sidewalk, and growing in this narrow crack was a dandelion plant. Many folks think dandelions are mere weeds, but to my professor and perhaps to other folk passing daily who took care not to step on it, it was a symbol of life's determination to thrive in the toughest of conditions.

The green leaves and yellow flowers were a spark of brightness and beauty that gave passersby a daily fillip of joy and hope as they noted, "It's still there!"

ANALYSIS

My professor's dandelion makes me think of the flowers I see growing by the roadside in and around my city — the pink and white swathes of cosmos at Easter-time, and the single sunflowers with their giant sunny heads that appear in small patches of ground between massive highway intersections. They make me happy!

And yet too often my attention is focused on the bad news coming through the car radio, or I'm grumbling about the traffic and bad driving habits of the motorists around me. I'm so stressed about everything I must still accomplish in the day that I seldom even notice the beautiful flowers, let alone devote a few minutes to what they may have to teach me, or the hope they might offer.

Are there horrors in the world? Yes. Do people do dreadful things to each other? Of course. Do we do daily damage to our planet? Yes, without a doubt.

But there are *also* wonderful, magnificent things. Supreme acts of courage and generosity. Works of beauty and creative genius that inspire. Small acts of kindness, and giant achievements in science, art and medicine.

The good stuff is not negated or invalidated by the bad.
You may have heard it said this way: all the darkness in the world cannot extinguish the light of a single candle.

It's critical that we truly *get* this. Just because terrible stuff happens, just because people are capable of cruelty, malice, negligence and stupidity, that does *not* mean that wonderful stuff doesn't *also* happen. People are capable of goodness, compassion, intelligence, mercy and gentleness. And love! (I sometimes think all the good stuff is just love manifesting in a million different ways, but that's a subject for another story.)

The good and the bad coexist. The thing is, it's been my experience that the world delivers horror stories fresh to your door. The bad news is the news that spreads fastest and widest — whether by gossip, formal news channels, or social media.

We need to *go out and find* the good stuff. We need to seek out beauty, recognize miracles when they happen, and be attuned to finding encouragement in the unlikeliest of places. We need to find and store up, like a squirrel with its nuts, those nuggets of goodness and kindness that we humans do show each other and our fellow species on this giant rock hurtling through space.

The world delivers bad news directly to your door.
You need to make a concerted effort to seek out the good news.

It turns out, you literally can train your brain to be on the lookout for certain stuff. Perhaps you've had that common experience of considering buying a certain make and model of car, and suddenly the roads and parking lots seem full of them? There aren't more about, it's just that your brain is more attuned to noticing them because they've suddenly become an object of interest to you.

Usually, your brain wants to warn you of dangers — that's why as a species we're naturally attuned to picking up on negative stuff. But you *can* train your attention to notice good things in the same way that the police might put out a *BOLO* — a be-on-the-lookout for a certain suspect or vehicle.

The reticular activation system is a set of connected nuclei located in the base of the human brain. It governs our arousal and awareness, and partly controls what sensory signals reach our conscious attention. It filters out unimportant incoming data received via our senses, and it decides whether something is important or unimportant based on what *we focus* on most.

If you choose to focus on the negative, you're literally training your brain to notice that more, to assign it higher importance, to collect more examples and evidence of how the world is a wretched and miserable place.

Train your brain to be on the lookout for the good,
happy, positive and beautiful.

If you make it a regular habit to seek out the positive, you'll train your brain to do more of this on your behalf. Good news stories will start grabbing your attention, you'll start seeing the silver lining in even negative experiences, you'll find it easier to practice gratitude, and the world will seem like a much happier, healthier, more hopeful place.

ACTION STEPS

1. Notice your own negative bias.

Become aware of how often you focus on the negative, and how often you repeat negative statements about the world, other people and yourself. Realize what this means: you are training your brain to stay stuck in a negative loop of noticing and reinforcing the worst.

2. Put out a *BOLO* for the positive.

Consciously and intentionally begin a habit of training your brain to notice the positive. Below, I've suggested some ways in which you can do this.

Every day, write down three things (big or small) that you're grateful for.

Try to notice one beautiful thing on the way to work.

Get out into nature (the wilds, or just a local park, or even your own back yard) and replenish your soul.

Stare up at the magnificence of the night sky.

Go to an art gallery and spend time in front of paintings and sculptures you find beautiful (not critiquing the ones you think are ugly).

Read inspirational books or listen to uplifting podcasts.

Read a beautiful poem.

Hug someone. Hug a pet.

Play music that makes you want to dance and sing. And dance and sing along!

Try, today, to notice fifty examples of beautiful or good things.

Challenge yourself to create some good in the world. Today, do five acts of random kindness for others, or do something that benefits the planet.

Catch the world doing something right! Notice how many drivers on that busy highway do signal before they change lanes, and do stay within the speed limit.

Be amazed at how all the planets stayed in alignment yesterday and will do so again tomorrow.

Instead of cursing the birdsong that wakes you early, lie and listen to the astonishing beauty of it.

Eat something you really like — a block of chocolate, a tender steak, a juicy peach. Eat it slowly and mindfully. Savor the taste and enjoy the experience.

Instead of saying, "I've got to bathe my kids and put them to bed," say, "I get to bathe my kids and put them to bed."

Pay attention to the parts of your body that are pain-free and in good working order.

Declare a good news day among your tribe on social media.

Examine the magnificence of a weed — its relentless persistence, its unapologetic "there-ness", its determination to survive.

Notice that wherever there is disaster, there is also kindness, altruism, generosity and heroism.

---

3. It doesn't come naturally.

These actions will feel false, unnatural and awkward at first. Persist! You've forced yourself to exercise physically before, haven't you? Did the exercise not count towards making you fitter and stronger because you had to *make* yourself do it? Of course not! It's the same with exercising your brain. Just do the work regularly, and watch the amazing results that follow.

4. It works in the short-term and the long-term.

Yes, it's a wonderful thing to enrich your life (and prolong it, too, according to research) by dwelling on the positive, the good and the beautiful in a general way. It becomes a part of your character over time. But the disciplined practice of noticing your dandelions in the sidewalk is also a short-term shot in the arm for a bad mood.

Next time you're feeling grumpy and mistreated, force yourself to spend fifteen minutes listing all the things you're grateful for in that moment, and watch what happens to your day and your mood.

5. Make and keep an ongoing list of the things that inspire, motivate, encourage and uplift you. Try to spend more time enjoying them.

THE TAKEAWAY

Make a habit of searching out the things that feed your soul, lift your heart and give you hope.
Train your brain to focus on the positive.

THE ONION AND THE
MACAROON

Do you ask for what you want? Or do you put up with what others give you? Are you able to say no to what you don't want?

THE STORY

I do a fair amount of training, some of it for organizations who wish to foster team spirit or clarify group dynamics, and some of it for groups of individuals wishing to improve their self-esteem, assertiveness, or counseling skills. And there's a game I usually get delegates to play during the course of the training.

I split the class into two (or more) groups and have them sit together in small circles on the floor. Then I deposit a closed grocery bag of edible substances into the center of each circle. Inside these bags are a mixture of nice and not so nice items. I include things most people would happily consume — cookies or a small cake, a chocolate or a bag of chips, a bottle of water, perhaps a miniature bottle of liqueur — but also some substances that many might find unpalatable, such as a can of tonic water, a chili pepper, super-sour jelly worms, and always a raw onion or potato. (We psychologists can be a little evil sometimes!)

I hold up a stopwatch and give the teams the following instructions:
The rules are that you must consume everything in the bag, within the time limit of exactly five minutes.

You may not talk.
You may not feed yourself.
The team who finishes first wins.
Your time begins... now! Go, go, go!

As everyone dives into the bags, and begins eating and feeding, I closely observe the individuals and the group dynamics. Who eats what? Who immediately grabs what items, and why? Who eats what they clearly don't like, and who refuses? Is there any group co-operation, any canvassing of preferences before the mania begins? Does anyone get upset or angry, and why? Which individuals simply refuse, with a determined shake of the head and lips pinched closed, to eat the gross items they are offered?

Surprisingly, it has never happened that an entire group refuses to play. I'm not sure what people think will happen if they break a rule in a training game. They can hardly anticipate dreadful consequences, and yet there always seems to be someone who eventually agrees to eat the inedible.

The time limit adds an element of urgency and fun to the game, but I also use it because time limits are stressful — and when we're stressed, we become more like ourselves, and our fault lines are more likely to show.

> *When we're under pressure, we become more like ourselves. What are you like when under stress?*

When the five minutes are up (or when it seems like things might be getting out of hand, usually when folks start eating the raw potato or onion), I call time, and we discuss what happened, unpacking the meaning for the individuals and the groups.

The first time I got a class to play this game must have been over fifteen years ago, but I still remember aspects of it very clearly. It was a class of adult students studying lay-counseling and they were wonderful, kind, empathic people with above-average insight into themselves. But that didn't stop one young man from rolling his raw potato into the other group's circle so that his group (or he himself?) didn't have to eat it.

The other group was clearly but silently outraged (no talking, remember?) and looked appealingly at me to veto this behavior. I shrugged and said, "It's not against the rules," fully expecting team two to toss the tuber back into the first group.

But that's not what happened. Astonishingly, team two kept the potato — and one person actually began eating it! Why, I wondered, did they do that? Were they seeking my approval for being the "good team", who didn't expect others to pick up their slack? Or were they just the sort of folks who kept the hand life dealt them?

A couple of the players immediately grabbed tasty items, then realized they couldn't feed themselves, and handed the items — a cookie, for example — over to a team mate, miming the request that the other person feed them. Although there was no obligation for the other person to do this, they almost always did, even though they could have fed the cookie to someone else in the group (or handed it back) and asked for it to be fed to themselves.

A couple of players grabbed what they themselves would like to eat, and then fed it to someone else. (I've played the game dozens of time, and this dynamic always happens.) On this occasion, in the team with the onion, and now also the potato, there were two interesting women. The younger of the two, who had the makings of a good therapist, was overweight and struggled with low self-esteem. The older was a woman in her late forties who had done the most remarkable work with refugees from war-torn countries in Africa.

As soon as the contents of the bag were revealed, the younger woman seized a delicious-looking macaroon and hung onto it. Clearly, she wished she could eat it but she was reluctant to let go of it, which was the only way she could get to eat it. Maybe she didn't trust others to feed her what she wanted if she asked, possibly she didn't believe she deserved the treat, or didn't want to be seen eating it in front of the others.

Whatever her motivation (I can no longer remember the exact reason), she fed the macaroon to the older woman. The older woman looked very reluctant to eat it, but when the younger pressed her, she complied.

When we discussed the game, it emerged that the older woman was a strict vegan for both health and ethical reasons, yet against her will, she had allowed herself to be force-fed something that not only revolted her, but was against her principles to eat.

"I'm sorry," the younger woman apologized, looking surprised by this revelation. "I thought you'd like the macaroon. Everyone likes macaroons, don't they?"

"No. I would rather have eaten the raw onion or the potato," the other replied.

ANALYSIS

This game is a quick and useful way to determine group dynamics, as well as some deep-seated individual beliefs and patterns of behavior. As I run through some of these dynamics below, try to figure out where you fit.

Some people believe they deserve the best and ask for it.

Some people don't believe they deserve the best.

Some people do their best to ensure that they get what they want, using fair means or foul.

Many people find it difficult to ask for what they want. Or perhaps it simply doesn't occur to them that they can.

Some people are pros at dumping undesirable tasks into the laps of other people.

Some people suck it up, even when it's not strictly necessary.

Some people are able to challenge the rules and stand up to authority, while others appear simply incapable of doing this.

Many, many people simply do what they are told.

Very few people stop, think, and plan before they act.

Some people find it so difficult to say no, to refuse or to disappoint others, that they wind up doing things they find unpalatable, unpleasant, offensive, or just plain wrong.

Some people think it's rude, selfish or even aggressive to state their needs or preferences.

Most people don't stop to ask what others prefer.

Many people give others what they want for themselves.

Some people are shirkers.

Some people are dutiful raw-potato eaters. There's a potato-eater in almost every group.

In life, the most you get is what you ask for.

Of course, you don't always get what you ask for, but one way to guarantee that you'll hardly ever get what you want is to make sure no one knows what it is you do want!

And one sure way to ensure you get force-fed what you *don't* want, is never to say, "No."

ACTION STEPS

These action steps are food for thought. I hope they challenge you to reassess some of your unhelpful (and unnecessary!) ways of thinking and behaving.

1. Saying no.

Can you — do you — ever say "no"? When, or with whom, is it particularly hard for you to say no? What is the cost of this to you?

2. Do you feed *others* what you secretly want for yourself? I'm not just talking here about tangible things, like macaroons. I'm also talking about things like encouragement, support, kindness, respect, and validation.

3. If you give others what you wish to receive, have you considered the idea that they may not want it?

4. Do you ask for what you want — do you literally put it into words and express it directly?

Other people don't know what you want unless you tell them. Stop expecting miracles of ESP and intuition, and don't assume that others will take the time and effort to ask you what you want. They very seldom do — not because they are monsters of selfishness, but simply because they are usually preoccupied with their own lives, needs and problems.

Ask for what you want. You may not get it. But by not asking, you are saying, "No" to the universe before you've even given it a chance to answer.

---

5. Remember, a request is neither a command nor a demand, and the other person is always free to turn you down.

Try saying:
I would like ...
I really want ...
I would prefer ...
I would rather not ...

These phrases are not rude or selfish or aggressive, though they may feel that way when you first start saying them because you have so little practice in stating your preferences. With practice, they'll come more easily.

6. Think about it from the other person's perspective — put yourself in their shoes for a moment. Wouldn't you rather give someone what they truly want? Yes? Well, how will you know what that is unless they tell you? The same applies to you.

> *When you ask for what you want, specifically and directly, you maximize your chances of getting it.*

7. Have you considered that asking for what you want allows other people the delight of giving it to you, that it provides them the soul-feeding joy of making another person (you) happy? It allows them to have a turn to take the moral high-ground, a chance to be the giver rather than the recipient, and to develop better and less selfish parts of themselves.

If you are always the giver, you effectively make others always the beneficiaries.

8. There are times when each of us needs to take one for the team, but if you are habitually your team, family, or social group's potato-eater, that's dysfunctional. It means you believe that you don't deserve better, or maybe you take pleasure from being a perpetual martyr.

If you always allow people to wipe their feet on you, don't be surprised when they begin to treat you as a doormat.

---

9. What's your relationship with people in authority — are you too compliant or perhaps unnecessarily defiant? What would you like to change about that dynamic? What do you truly want to be allegiant to? Try to pinpoint specific values, or principles (for example, justice, compassion, honesty), rather than particular people or positions of authority.

THE TAKEAWAY

In life, the most you get is what you ask for. Start asking for what you want.
Also, stop giving others what you want. Give them what they'd prefer instead.

WHEN MARS GOES ROGUE

Are you trying to change some aspect of yourself? Are other people resisting your change or labeling it negatively? Read on to find out how you're like Mars gone rogue.

THE STORY

We live on a beautiful blue planet in the solar system, in which all the planets revolve obediently around the sun, the star at the center of our system. Many of the planets, earth among them, are in turn orbited at regular intervals by their own moons, and comets orbit through our system — mostly on a predictable timetable, following the same route each time. Each planet continues to rotate at the same speed and maintains the same distance from the sun and from other planets in the system. It's all very ordered and predictable. The entire system is in a harmonious equilibrium.

But it wasn't always like this!

There was a time when the universe was new, when our star was being born, and when the Milky Way was more chaotic. Planets, moons, asteroids and comets must have bounced off each other like wild balls in a crazy pinball machine, leaving massive dents in planetary surfaces, sending each other careening into new orbits, possibly even bumping celestial bodies into trajectories which sent them straight into the sun to be sizzled up.

It was only over time (*eons* of time) that things eventually settled down into the calmer, predictable patterns we know today. And, having finally found a geographical setup, and patterns of movement which minimize collisions, our solar system is very resistant to change. Everything is held in check in a precise, balanced arrangement of movement and stability.

Now just imagine that one day, the planet Mars decided to go rogue. What if Mars thought, "Why do I always have to be the one so close to the sun? It's hot here, man! Look at earth over there with its water and its trees and its life — no fair! I want to get me some of that. I'm going to change my orbit today. Wheee!"

What if Mars took off in a new direction, orbited the sun at a different distance, or perhaps decided it would rather orbit Earth instead — what would happen then?

There would be another long, crazy period of chaos — more crashes, friction, and adjustments. The changes would ripple out through the entire solar system, affecting all bodies individually, and the arrangement and pattern of movement as a whole, even though just one planet had changed its position. Presumably those planets closest to Mars would be the most affected.

The planets and comets would be in different orbits and that would have implications for the length of their days and years. It might even impact on the existence of life on our own earth if we were bumped out of our perfect Goldilocks Zone and into an orbit closer to or farther away from the sun. It could quite possibly mean the extinction of life as we know it.

If our planets had minds and volition, they'd probably try to pressure Mars back into its usual spot in the grand scheme of things, in the hope that the old status quo would be restored, and they themselves would have to make fewer adjustments. If Mars refused to go back and persisted in its new course, it would take another few collision-riddled eons of disharmony and change before a new equilibrium finally established itself.

By now, you're probably thinking Mars is the baddie in this story –

the non-conformist planet that upsets all the others for purely selfish reasons. But what if Mars is trying to change for the better?

ANALYSIS

Our solar system resists change.
Human systems do, too.

Human systems are groups of people bonded together in some way, like families or organizations. There are also smaller subsystems (the married couple or the sibling subsystems in a family; departments or work teams in an organization), and bigger supra-systems (an extended family or cultural group; or an international organization or economic system).

Over time, with enough interactions between them, these systems establish some kind of balance. By "balance" in this context, I don't mean health. I mean that each member finds their place, and that certain ways of behaving and interacting dominate and are seen as "normal" in that system.

If your boss, let's call her Linda, always arrives late and hungover at work, that's not "balanced" in the "healthy" sense of the word. But it is predictable, even expected. The other members of your work system will find ways to work with this, around it, compensate for it, or even benefit from it.

The boss's assistant, Alison, might immediately bring Linda a strong cup of coffee and a couple of headache tablets. Saabir, the sales manager, will always schedule his meetings with Linda in the afternoon when her headache has lifted. Tom, from technical support, will know it's safe to arrive late for work because the boss is never there to check up on him, and Penny, from payroll, may find ways to line her pockets because boss Linda is too muzzy to thoroughly audit the financials.

Now imagine Linda changes. She gets help with her addiction, attends AA meetings regularly, stops drinking, and starts coming to work bright and early, clear-headed and eager to manage her department efficiently.

Because Linda has changed, everyone else will need to change, too. Alison might be delighted and Saabir relieved, but the others would be a lot less enthusiastic because, not only would they need to adapt, but they would have to adapt in directions which didn't suit them. Tom would have less free time and Penny less money. And if Linda really started digging, those two might even lose their jobs.

Here's a likely scene that might play itself out one Friday afternoon, at five o'clock.

The team start putting on their jackets and Tom says to Linda, "Hey boss, we're all going out for an after-work drink. Come join us."

"Not this time, but thanks for the invitation," Linda replies.

"Aw, why not? It won't be the same without you."

"Yeah, who'll get us laughing if you're not there?" Penny adds.

Linda shakes her head. "No, thanks."

"Don't be such a spoilsport — it's Alison's birthday, and the whole team should be there to celebrate," Tom urges.

"I said no," Linda answers.

"Well, no need to be rude," Tom says in a wounded tone.

"I'm not being rude. I just don't want to go."

"Okay, okay, no need to get angry! If you don't want to spend time with your team, just say so."

"I'm not angry!" By now Linda is red-faced and shouting. "And I *do* want to spend time with you guys, just not at a bar."

"Well, I think it's a big ask to expect all of us to stop drinking just because you have," Penny says. "Why don't you come with and you can just have a soft drink?"

"All right!" Linda finally concedes.

They all troop off to the bar, the very last place a recovering alcoholic should be hanging out. What do you think happens there?

When we change ourselves, it affects others in ways
they may not like.

Whenever we try to transform some important aspect of ourselves, it impacts on others and requires *them* to change in order to adapt to *our* new ways. People find change — even positive change — to be challenging, and so they tend to avoid and resist it. When they are required to change in ways that they don't regard as personally advantageous, they're likely to resist even harder.

Some of the ways in which you might change which would affect your family include things such as:

You spend less time vegging in front of the TV and more time exercising.

You want to be less of a doormat, and so you become more assertive.

You start studying for a degree.

You change your job.

You get a paid job when you have been a stay-at-home parent until now.

You ask your family to help more with the chores at home.

You move to another house or city.

You insist on having more say in the family's finances.

You request a raise or promotion at work.

You stop smoking, drinking or drugging.

You start socializing more, or less.

Your aging, ailing parent comes to live with you.

You start challenging prejudice by calling out people who make racist or sexist jokes around you.

You lose a lot of weight.

You want the abuse in your relationship to stop, so you ask your partner to attend couples counselling with you.

You ask for a divorce.

You have another baby.

You want the family to start eating healthier, or you yourself want to become a vegetarian (or stop being one).

Can you see how any of these changes would require the whole family to adapt? Each member, as well as how the family system behaves and interacts as a whole, would need to change.

As with our colliding planets when Mars went rogue, there would be a period of chaos — misunderstandings and miscommunication, unmet expectations, disagreements, friction, tears, laughter and fights.

And the system (the family system in this case) would resist change. You would encounter pushback intended (consciously or unconsciously) to get you back in your lane so things would return to the way they were before.

Systemic resistance from others can take many forms:

Anger

(*Who do you think you are? What gives you the right to decide this? Just stop!*)

Rejection

(*I don't like this new you. I preferred you the way you were. Oh, just go away.*)

Stigmatizing, labelling

(*You're mad. You're selfish. You're wrong. You're possessed by the devil.*)

Minimizing

(*You're being silly. This isn't necessary. You're being over-sensitive.*)

Questioning, undermining

(*Who put this idea in your head? Don't you think things were better for all of us before?*)

Threats of abandonment

(*Well if that's the way things are going to be in the future, I don't think we have a future. I don't see how this can work. If I'd wanted someone who was like this, I would have married him/her.*)

Sabotage

(*For example, keeping alcohol in the house of a recovering alcoholic and drinking in front of them, or even spiking their soft drink with a shot of alcohol; offering someone who's given up smoking "just one" cigarette; going out for a family dinner at a junk food restaurant where there are no healthy options when one member goes on a diet, etc.*)

Refusal
(*I won't! No!*)
Violence

ACTION STEPS

1. When you embark on changing yourself, expect systemic resistance (pushback from those around you.)

2. Prepare for this resistance by explaining to those closest to you why and how you'll be changing, and why it's important to you. Ask them how they think it might impact on them, and see if you can find ways to deal with that constructively. Explicitly ask for their support.

3. If you still get resistance (and you probably will, even if others don't deliberately intend to sabotage your progress), then you have a decision to make — you can either give in or persist.

If you have carefully considered your new way of being, and truly believe it to be better and healthier, then you owe it to yourself to stick out the change. What usually happens is that if you persist in your new "orbit", after a while the members in the system eventually begin to adapt, and the chaos and conflict settle down. A new pattern of interaction is established, and the changed ways become the new status quo.

Give the system time to adapt to the change. Try to show how the change ultimately benefits everybody.

---

4. Sometimes, however, others have a vested interest in trying to force things back to how they were. They believe that they have too much to lose by changing or by allowing you to change, and their resistance increases in strength or nastiness. Then you need to consider whether you can still be a member of that system, whether it's possible to be a healthy member of a dysfunctional unit.

When someone gives up alcohol or drugs, for example, they usually wind up leaving or changing many of their friendship circles. The social group's old way of socializing was built around going out to party and get drunk, and when one member becomes a teetotaler, the others feel uncomfortable. They believe they are being judged, and exert such pressure on the sober person that he or she either falls off the wagon, or leaves the group.

Some systems are extremely resistant to change. If you are in a relationship characterized by domestic violence, for example, and your partner is unwilling or unable to change, you need to leave. (*Please get expert support to do this in the safest way possible*).

5. Put the shoe on the other foot for a moment. Consider the groups of which you are a member and how you may be resisting change in *others*. How can you rather support the health-directed change of your friends, family and colleagues? How can you stay flexible, and adapt more easily to the inevitable changes in your home or work environment?

THE TAKEAWAY

Whenever you change, you are likely to be met with resistance because a change in you demands that those around you also adapt.

Don't give up on your change too soon just because of a bit of friction or resistance. Persist and be consistent, and give the system time to make the necessary adjustments.

THE LABRADOR AND THE SCORPION

Do you get hurt, betrayed, let down, or exploited over and over again? Sometimes even by the same person? Do you fall for charming manipulation and emotional blackmail, even when your common sense tells you to run a mile? If your answers are "yes," then this story is for you.

THE STORY

There are many versions of this story, which may have originated in Aesop's Fable of the farmer and the viper, or in an ancient Sanskrit folk tale of a turtle and a scorpion. In one version, the main characters are a frog and a scorpion.

My version involves a dog, which I have always pictured to be a golden Labrador, because they are the most gentle and good-natured of breeds, and I can just imagine them getting into a pickle because they struggle to imagine that others could have less pure motives than themselves.

Once upon a time, the story goes, a scorpion wanted to cross a river that was in flood, but being a poor swimmer, he asked a dog to carry him across.

The dog, very surprised at this request, protested, "Why on earth would I do that? You are venomous, and we are mortal enemies. Your kind kills my kind."

"My dear friend," the scorpion chuckled, "I would never do that. If I sting you while we are crossing the river, you would sink and drown, and I would perish right along with you! And once you got me to the other side, I would be so grateful for your assistance, that I could never hurt you."

This made perfect sense to the dog, so he crouched down and allowed the scorpion to crawl up onto the top of his head. The dog paddled across the swollen river, feeling good about how he was doing a great favor to the scorpion. When they reached the opposite bank, the exhausted dog lowered his head so that his passenger could climb off, but as it did so, the scorpion gave the dog a mighty sting.

Dying, the dog looked at the scorpion in sad confusion and, with his last breath groaned, "But I did you a great service. I saved your life, and now you have taken mine. Why?"

The scorpion shrugged and said, "I am a scorpion — it is my nature. You knew what I was when you met me."

Some people, like some creatures, are dangerous.

ANALYSIS

Some people exploit, abuse, manipulate, and cause harm to others. It is in their character to behave this way, and they make no great effort to overcome this base nature. Usually, they do not even acknowledge that there's anything wrong with the way they treat others.

The dog in the story knows the scorpion is dangerous when he first sees it, but *we* may not immediately recognize who, and what, these toxic people are. They often come across as very charming, intelligent and charismatic — initially, at least. They flatter us, and we feel special when they love-bomb us with attention and praise. We feel chosen. We either don't see, or choose not to recognize, the stinger that is an essential part of their makeup.

But they can't keep up the pretense forever, and soon their true nature begins to reveal itself.

These people show us who they are by how they behave towards others.

They often treat those with less power (such as restaurant servers) badly, but schmooze up to those with a higher status. Their relationships are based on what they think they can get for themselves from the other. They frequently have a string of stormy personal relationships behind them, and always blame their exes for the failures, framing themselves as innocent victims.

These people show us who they are by what they do.

They have often failed at a succession of businesses, or have repeatedly been fired from their jobs. They may have been blacklisted on credit sites due to bad debt, or crossed paths with the law.

They cheat on their partners, their taxes, their employers. They borrow money from friends and family and don't pay it back. They sway recovering addicts from the path of sobriety. They let their business partners do all the work. They steal — money, ideas, time and confidence. They get enraged, destructive, or violent when embarrassed, challenged, or denied what they desire.

If you look, you will see a definite lack of empathy, and a distinct pattern of disregard for the rights of others.

Long before they veer into the territory of full-on verbal abuse, they start with critical, hurtful comments, or ones which undermine your self-confidence. They say:

Do you really think you should eat dessert?

I think that job might be too difficult for you.

Wow, Betty doesn't seem to have a problem keeping her kids in line.

Long before they start hitting, kicking, or throttling their "beloved" partners, they punch walls and mirrors, throw objects, push and shove their partners, abandon them in restaurants midway through a meal, or punish them with days of silence.

Before they start sexually molesting children, they usually groom them — online or in person — taking an exceptional interest in a child, wanting to spend alone time with them (often in situations which involve undress), and entangling the child in wrong behavior like drinking alcohol or watching pornography.

These people even tell us straight out who they are.

They say:

I don't believe in monogamy.

I like a drink.

I'm very competitive.

If someone wrongs me, I won't rest until I've paid them back with interest.

I think a man should head up the relationship.

I prefer to stick to friends of my own color.

I believe in keeping a strict rein on the family finances.

If you ever looked at another man, I'd kill you, ha ha.

We translate their actual words into a more benign version, telling ourselves:

He's philosophically interesting, a deep thinker who challenges convention.

She's a cultured lady who appreciates wine.
He has a strong sense of justice, and is a natural leader.
He's picky — that doesn't mean he's a racist.
She's not miserly. She's just careful with money.
Ooh, he's a little jealous; that must mean he really loves me!

When someone shows or tells you who they are, believe them.

In our gut, we may know who they are when we employ them or date them or — heaven help us — marry them, but we tell ourselves that with *us*, it will be different. *We* will rescue, fix, or change them.

If you are a Labrador sort of person — one who takes responsibility for your own behavior, who tries to do the right thing and to help others, if you are a little naïve and tend to ascribe the best motives to even the worst behavior of others — then good for you! You're probably an honest, kind, loyal person, and I don't want you to change.

But for your own health and well-being, please stop picking up scorpions. I know they can be fascinating, that the element of unpredictability and potential danger adds a certain spice, but you will *not* change them. They are scorpions by nature.

Start seeing scorpions for what they are — dangerous creatures who can't be tamed, or changed, or turned into pet rabbits.

Scorpions make dangerous pets. Although some aren't venomous, unless you're an expert, it's difficult to tell those apart from the lethal species. And they all sting — sometimes it just hurts, other times it can kill you. Sometimes you don't react badly to the first sting, but the fifth or the fiftieth can trigger a potential fatal allergic reaction.

In the same way, if you align yourself with a scorpion, as friend, partner or colleague, sooner or later you're going to get hurt. And it could be fatal. In the vast majority of homicides where the victim is female, for example, the perpetrator is either a current or ex intimate partner, or a friend or relative of that partner.

ACTION STEPS

1. See the danger.

When a person behaves in a way that shocks you, because it reveals something dark or wrong or dangerous about their nature, please don't write it off as a once-off occurrence, and don't assume that all is well because they apologize.

Nothing is more common than for an abuser or a thief or an addict to apologize profusely and with seemingly genuine remorse. But nothing is more common than for the same behavior to occur again and again. And the longer you stay stuck in this repeating dysfunctional pattern, the harder it is to break free.

Apologies are easy.
Without behavior change, they count for nothing.

---

2. Beware the rose-tinted spectacles.

You may be in love, in lust, or really drawn to this new person and the opportunities they promise, but take off those rose-tinted spectacles and see what actually *is* rather than what you wish was there. Acknowledge the reality behind the charming sales patter. Look for the *pattern of behavior* over time and across different relationships and contexts. Anyone can make a mistake, but these people consistently leave damage in their wake, and they always blame others.

Assess the potential dangers and pitfalls in any enterprise or relationship (business, friendship, or intimate) and don't be in a rush to trust blindly. If there are red flags early on, decline to go any further.

It's easier to say "no" to scorpions and flooded rivers than it is to recover from a venomous sting or from drowning.

---

3. Get help getting out.

If you are already in a relationship characterized by abuse, violence, or other serious dysfunction, please get professional help. There are many resources, which you can easily find online, with knowledgeable people to assist you. You do not have to do this alone, and you do not have to stay stuck.

4. Remind yourself that you cannot change another.

If you have just met a scorpion, do not fall for his or her tricks. Often, when we see that the other person is damaged, we see the hurt, sadness and fear lying deep beneath the anger. And there is hurt — abusers were often themselves abused as children.

But a relationship is not therapy. You cannot change or fix this person. You need to save yourself.

A relationship is not therapy.

---

5. What if you believe they can change themselves?

If you care deeply for someone and they swear they will change (change *themselves* — have you heard me when I tell you that no person can change another?), step away and give them the time and space to effect that change. Encourage them to get whatever professional help they need in healing and changing. If, one day, they have transformed into a healthier creature (it is rare, but it can happen), then you can build a new relationship with them at that time.

6. You may have noticed that my analysis and action steps are directed to those who are the victims or potential victims, rather than to the perpetrators — to the Labradors, in other words, rather than to the scorpions. The reason for this is that perpetrators seldom seek help, because they do not take responsibility for their actions. They do not genuinely even see that their conduct is wrong, because they lack empathy. They lack the capacity to understand the destructive and painful impact of their manipulative, exploitative, or abusive actions on others. They blame their victims, and in time, victims begin to blame themselves.

Like the scorpion in the story, perpetrators themselves seldom suffer as a result of their actions. After all, a scorpion is well armored and well camouflaged. It does not sting itself, and even if it did, it would be immune to its own venom.

THE TAKEAWAY

As American poet, writer and civil rights activist Maya Angelou famously advised, "When people show you who they are, believe them the first time."

A CHILD AT THE WHEEL

If your life were a moving car, who would be behind the wheel?

THE STORY

When I was about three or four years old, an incident happened which could have ended tragically.

I had been sitting up front with my father in his pickup truck, when he parked it in the street in front of our house. That house was located halfway up a steep hill, and the street ended in a T-junction at the bottom of the hill where an extremely busy main thoroughfare ran by. Beyond that main road, the ground dipped away sharply down an embankment to the sports fields of the local university.

My father stepped out of the truck for just a moment — to collect something from the house, I think, no-one remembers the details. I'd been watching him change gears on the gear stick which protruded from the steering wheel, and lift and lower the handbrake, and turn the wheel. Driving a car looked like such fun! I wanted to try it, too.

I don't remember exactly what I did but from the results, I'm guessing that I must have lowered the handbrake and somehow shifted the car into gear, or perhaps neutral. At once, the car began moving, and catastrophe — for me and for others — was mere seconds away.

I think a guardian angel was watching me that day, because instead of rolling down the hill, hitting pedestrians or children in the street, careering into the four lanes of the busy main road at the bottom of the hill, or nose-diving over the embankment beyond, the truck moved forward a little and then veered sideways — straight into the neighbor's wall.

It had picked up enough speed to knock over a section of wall (which my father later had to rebuild for the neighbor), but it came to an abrupt halt. I was a little shocked, my parents understandably upset, the neighbor grumpy about his wall, but — miraculously — no one had been hurt or killed.

This is the kind of accidental destruction that occurs when a kid is behind the wheel.

ANALYSIS

Would you go for a ride if a four-year-old was driving?

Would you buckle up in an aircraft if your pilot was a seven-year-old? Would you sign up for surgery if a ten-year-old child was doing the operation? Would you hand over your finances, health, emotional well-being, or relationships to a kid for him or her to manage? No? I didn't think so. You'd be a fool to do it, and I know you're not a fool.

And yet ... who is behind the wheel of your life? Is it a childlike part of yourself?

Each of us had significant experiences in our childhood. Some were good, and some were bad. Unfortunately, it's the bad experiences that leave the deepest mark. We are like Velcro for the negative and Teflon for the positive. If you don't believe me, just notice how you react differently to receiving praise versus criticism. Which sticks harder and longer?

There are neurological reasons for this — the primitive and powerful parts of our brain want us to remember bad and dangerous things (saber-toothed tigers, poisonous berries, the leader of the tribe reprimanding us), so that we can try to avoid them in the future.

Added to this is the fact that when we have strongly negative experiences as a child, we assume it's our fault. Again, there's a neurological reason for this. Our role-taking capacity (the ability to put ourselves in someone else's position and imagine the world from their perspective, to guess at their feelings and motivations) is not fully developed until adolescence.

When a teacher yells, "You're useless at math!" at a child, the child is likely to swallow that belief. *Teacher says it, so it must be true, right? Teacher is speaking about me. I'm dumb at math.*

The child is likely to act in accordance with this new belief, and, in a self-fulfilling prophecy, develop a mental block about the subject and perform badly.

If a grumpy teacher yells the same thing at a teenager, the teen is more likely (or at least cognitively able) to think, *I wonder what bug crawled up teacher's butt this morning? Teacher is speaking junk. What do they know about me?*

They realize the teacher's mood and words are, to some degree at least, influenced by himself — his irritated state of mind, something else that is happening in his life, his frustrations with teaching today, or perhaps even his insecurities about his ability to explain the subject adequately.

Note, in the teenage example, I say teenagers are *more likely* to shrug off the negative label, not *guaranteed.* This is because teens (and adults) who have had multiple experiences of being told how inferior or inadequate they are, are much more likely to uncritically swallow new negative messages, and believe them to be true of themselves.

I've taught my children and my clients this little idiom: *what other people say and do, reflects on them and not on you.* It speaks of their character, their manners, morals and mood, not yours. But sadly, most children don't know this.

What other people say and do reflects on them and not on you.

So, based on the negative experiences of childhood (sexual, physical, or emotional abuse; bullying and/or negative labeling; traumatic experiences; abandonment; neglect; parental death or divorce; serious illnesses or hospitalizations; accidents big and small), most people enter adulthood having internalized negative or dysfunctional beliefs.

These beliefs may be about others or the world, for example:

The world is a dangerous place.

Other people don't like or want me.

Money doesn't grow on trees.

It's every man for himself in this life.

Men are pigs / women are inferior.

Or these beliefs may be about yourself, for example:

I'm stupid. I'm no good at science.

I'm fat, ugly, too tall, too short.

I'm uncreative. I can't draw or paint. I'm bad at dancing.

I'm dirty, bad, worthless, unlovable.

I'm weak, sickly.

I'll always be alone.

I deserve to be treated badly, punished, experience pain.

I can't trust others.

I'm a failure. I'll never amount to much.

These beliefs lead you to make critical decisions — rules about how to function in the world. These "decisions" can be conscious, or you might be unaware of them. They may lurk in your subconscious, steering your behaviors and your life in a form of dysfunctional autopilot. Here are some examples of such default beliefs:

I'd better make myself useful because although nobody could ever truly want me, I can make myself needed. I should hook up with an addict or a "rough diamond" because then I'll always be needed.

Hurt them before they hurt you. I'd better screw up the relationship before they have a chance to reject or abandon me.

If I make myself unattractive, for example through obesity, then no one will date me, and if no one dates me, no one can dump me and I'll never be hurt like that again.

I'll never be rich, so there's no point in saving. I may as well spend and enjoy.

But do you see what has happened? You're living your life based on decisions you made as a kid.

If you're living your life according to decisions you made as a child, then a child is behind the wheel of your life.

The child who is molested, for example, believes what she is told (*I'm dirty; I must keep this a secret or he'll kill/leave my mother; he gave me money and sweets so I've been paid for this which means I kinda asked for it*). He or she doesn't think the more accurate thoughts (*This man is a pedophile who should be reported and brought to justice. He's probably done this to scores of other children. He only picked on me because I was accessible.*)

As an adult, those beliefs still lurk: *I'm dirty, I can't tell anyone my shameful secret, I'm morally bad.*

Now that we're adults, we need to understand that as children we weren't capable of understanding the mind and motives of others. We need to have compassion for who we were back then, and understand that our responses were our best efforts to cope with what was happening.

We need to appreciate that the beliefs we internalized were an attempt to help make sense of the world and of what was happening to us. But, we also need to haul those dysfunctional and false beliefs up out of the well of our subconscious, and re-examine them in the light of adult reason, logic, experience, and knowledge. We need to rewrite the beliefs so that they are more accurate, more constructive, more likely to support us in being healthy and happy.

When you were a child, you didn't know any better. Now that you're an adult who knows better, who's experienced more of life, who understands a lot more about what makes others tick, it's time to critically analyze your default settings and rewrite the code that governs you.

It's time to put your intelligent, informed, adult self behind the wheel of your life.

ACTION STEPS

1. Identify your dysfunctional beliefs.

Take a piece of lined paper and fold it in half vertically. At the top of the left-hand side, write *Experiences*, and at the top of the right-hand side, write *Beliefs*.

In the left-hand column, make a list of traumatic things, people or events you experienced as a child. Leave several lines of space between items, and aim to remember at least seven.

These can be "traumatic" with a small "t" (for example, your ballet teacher told you that you were too big to be a dancer, dad said he didn't have enough money for you to go on the school history tour, you dropped your glass of milk and your mother yelled at you that you were clumsy), or they can be Traumatic with a capital T (for example, you were sexually abused, your father died in a car accident in which you were a passenger, your mother was an alcoholic who beat you and your siblings). They may have been once-off events, or they may have taken months or even years (for example, parental conflict and divorce proceedings, long-term bullying), or your entire childhood (for example, poverty or war).

In the column on the right-hand side, opposite each experience, list the belief/s you think you developed based on that experience. In addition to deciding on something about yourself, check whether you also perhaps constructed a belief about the world, about other people, or about the issue at hand (such as money, food, the opposite sex, trust, love, etc.)

2. Take a moment to acknowledge that as a child, you did the best you were able. Find a quiet moment, sit comfortably, breathe deeply and, in your mind's eye, imagine that young, helpless, scared and hurt child that once was you.

Gently tell him or her: *Thank you for coping with that for me. I know you did the best you were able, and it must have helped because I survived. Thank you. But I'm big now, and it's time for me to take charge, so I'm going to be changing the way I think and behave so that it's better for us, okay?*

Imagine yourself deliberately and consciously getting back into your adult state, take a deep breath, and come back to the present here and now.

3. Critically — with your adult brain — examine the beliefs from childhood.

Are they true?

Are they still true — now at this present time in your life?

Are they functional, or do they lead you to live a life which is smaller, unhealthier, sadder or less successful?

What does it cost you (in time, energy, money, joy, health, relationships, spiritual connection) to keep hanging onto these beliefs?

Have these beliefs outlived their usefulness? In other words, are you clutching at old, outdated, past-their-expiration-date beliefs that need to be tossed?

4. Rewrite the beliefs so that they are more constructive and accurate.

So, *I'm stupid* becomes *I'm strong and smart.*

I'm dirty may become *I'm good. He was the one with the problem.*

I was born poor and I'll die poor might become *Every day I manage my money better.*

I'm worthless becomes *I'm a good person. I deserve love and respect.*

It's my fault my parents got divorced may become *It had nothing to do with me. They were adults, and their relationship problems were their responsibility.*

5. Start living your life in line with your new settings.

Note: It's not necessary that you wholeheartedly *believe* these new ideas about yourself — yet. After all, you've been living with the old beliefs for years and years. But it is necessary that you start becoming more aware. Catch yourself when you behave in accordance with the old rule, and consciously try to live in line with the new one.

Ask yourself:

What would a smart person do here?

If I wasn't dirty or shameful, how do I want to feel about, and start treating, my body?

If I'm a person who manages money effectively, do I really want to sign up for a new store card and more debt?

If I'm a good person who deserves love and respect, what do I need to do about the fact that my partner emotionally abuses and cheats on me?

Then act in line with new and improved beliefs.

THE TAKEAWAY

Don't let the damaged child run your life. Put your adult self behind the wheel, and start steering!

RED KETTLE SURPRISE

Do you sometimes hold back from doing something kind or good because what you can give is too small to make a real difference? I hope this true story, which is one of my favorites, will open your heart and change your mind about that.

THE STORY

Every year, as the festive season approaches, the US Salvation Army stations volunteers at key shopping spots. They ring their bells, inviting passersby to drop donations into their distinctive red kettles. The money gathered is used to fund a multitude of good causes: winter coats and Christmas gifts for children, daily hot meals for the hungry, overnight shelter for thousands of homeless people on the streets in winter, plus hundreds of thousands of bags of groceries and clothing donations to the poor.

November 2015 was just the same, and yet it was wonderfully different. That year, someone quietly deposited a check for $500,000 into a collection kettle outside a grocery store in Twin Cities, Minnesota. The check cleared, but when the charity contacted them, the donors insisted on keeping their identities under wraps, rather than going public with their act of great generosity.

The benefactors, it turned out, were a local couple and were long-time supporters of the charity, though this was their largest donation to date. The couple told the Salvation Army that they had at one time lived on scraps of discarded food, knew what it was like to go hungry, and wanted to encourage others to be generous, too.

The reason why they had chosen to make their donation to the poor via the Salvation Army, lay in distant history. One of their fathers had served in the trenches in World War I and had always remained grateful to the "doughnut lassies" of the Salvation Army who delivered free coffee, doughnuts and water to the fighting soldiers. For the couple, their donation was a way to thank those volunteers, to honor their fathers, and to give to the less fortunate.

"You get to a point in life where it's time to take care of others, the way you were taken care of," the donors said in an anonymous statement to the press.

ANALYSIS

Did any of the volunteers back in World War I ever wonder what the heck they were doing out there on the frontlines? I'd be willing to bet that the doughnut lassies were often warned to rather stay home, where it was safer. I'm sure the thought must have crossed their minds that they were doing so little, in such wretched conditions where the soldiers were suffering all manner of injuries and indignities, that their efforts were insignificant. Many times, it must have felt like they weren't making a difference — not one that mattered, anyway.

And yet, turning a doughnut and a cup of coffee into $500,000 that will benefit tens of thousands of people, and possibly inspire others to give more? That's some return on investment!

None of us can know the impact of our acts of kindness. We cannot foresee how a single considerate or helpful act causes ripples which spread out in the present and even reach way into the future. We don't know how many others might be inspired by our behavior to do good of their own.

---

*The impact of a good deed ripples out across the
present and deep into the future.*

I believe that kindness is one of the most powerful virtues, and one of the most under-rated. A smile, a kind word, a helping hand at the right time — these can literally save lives. And you don't need to be on the battlefront to do it.

Everyone you meet today is going through something you know nothing about. And that might be the reason some of them are behaving in less than pleasant ways. They are carrying wounds and worries, just as you are. And you have the power to decide whether to help lighten their load, or add to their burden.

Every act of kindness, understanding and generosity you give into the world grows and multiplies — as does every act of unkindness, discrimination, judgement and withholding. Hurt people, hurt people. Angry people, anger people.

The good news is that when you act out the qualities you would like to see more of in the world, you will find that not only does it benefit others, it directly impacts on *your own* health and happiness.

---

*Doing good for others directly benefits them **and you**!*

At a neurochemical level, doing good deeds for others (especially actions that require some effort or sacrifice on your part) results in the secretion of dopamine in your brain. This chemical is involved in our feelings of love, trust, emotional warmth and safety. But not only does it result in you feeling good, it also boosts your immune system, inhibits addiction, increases your goal-directed behavior, and improves creativity!

Helping others less fortunate than yourself forces you to "compare down." In our busy, competitive lives, we're always "comparing up" —

measuring ourselves against those who are richer, fitter, stronger, or more successful, attractive, or popular than ourselves. Spend some time with folks who have much less, and watch how your own feelings of gratitude rise. Happiness isn't only about getting what you want, it's also about learning to be content, and a healthy sense of gratitude increases contentment.

Gratitude increases contentment.

When you give, you define yourself as someone who has a surplus of that commodity. If you can afford to give it away, then you are by definition rich — in money, time, skill, energy, compassion, or whatever it is that you're donating.

This is excellent therapy for *yourself*, because it challenges those limiting beliefs you keep brainwashing yourself with — *I have no money, I'm too busy, I'm tired, I'm not good at anything, nobody wants me, I've got nothing to give.*

It forces you to realize you have an abundance to give. And when you believe yourself to be rich, blessed, lucky, the universe has a way of helping you manifest that. (This is the happy flip side of the negative self-fulfilling prophecy, in which you believe yourself to be poor, unwanted, stupid, etc., and find yourself living out that way of being.)

Research shows that being kind to others makes you feel better about yourself, and formalizing your kindness into regular volunteering brings even greater benefits. You already know that helping others benefits those on the receiving end, but perhaps you didn't know that many studies have confirmed that volunteering is correlated with increased happiness, self-esteem, better physical and mental health, and reduced stress and illness *in the volunteer.* Turns out, it's good to be good!

ACTION STEPS

1. Volunteer.

Offer to help some person, charity or organization you care about. A donation of money is always welcome, but it's when you give of yourself — your time, effort, attention and thoughtfulness — that the benefits really begin to flow.

Here are a few volunteering ideas:

Help out at a soup kitchen or community vegetable garden.

Volunteer for a literacy project, or to entertain children in a hospital, or to spend time with old folks at the retirement home.

Build a house with Habitat for Humanity.

Teach someone how to sew, bake, or master some skill they can use to earn an income.

Volunteer at an animal shelter, or raise awareness on an environmental project.

Pick up litter in your neighborhood.

Support a family who's fallen on hard times with extra groceries.

Join (or create) a group at your local library that helps children with their homework.

Use your skills to help improve unemployed people's chances of landing employment by typing up a resume, or conducting a training workshop on job interview skills or telephone etiquette.

Donate your toiletry samples from hotel visits and airline bags to homeless shelters.

Run in a road race to raise funds or awareness for a worthy cause.

Volunteer your time at a local charity to help in any way they need.

Babysit for a parent who needs a break. Volunteer to do respite care for families with special needs members, so they can have some time out to rest and recharge.

Give blood to the blood bank.

Sign up to become an organ donor so that even after your death, you keep giving.

There are endless ways to help. Pick a cause you care about deeply (children, animals, literacy, or fighting cancer, for example), or — to really grow your soul — choose a cause that will be difficult for you (working at an AIDS hospice or with the aged, for example), and simply begin helping.

Begin today.

2. Be kind

Make it a daily habit to do random acts of kindness. Here are just a few examples:

Smile at the cashier, the librarian, the person who picks up litter or checks your train ticket.

Pay someone a compliment. (Note, I don't mean hit on someone. "Hey sexy lady, you've got a cute butt," is not a compliment, it's sexual harassment.)

Say thank you, even when you don't need to.

Make or buy a meal for someone who needs it.

Clear out your books, clothes, and other belongings, and donate what you don't need or no longer use to a local library, charitable shop or shelter.

Allow a fellow motorist to move into the traffic ahead of you.

Send a snail-mail card (so rare these days!) with a kind message of appreciation to an older relative.

Pay for a stranger's coffee. Some coffee shops now allow you to buy a "suspended coffee" which a needy person can later claim for free.

Buy a pot plant, or even just put a single flower in a soda bottle, and pop it on a colleague's desk when no one is looking.

If you are religious, say a prayer for someone you know is going through a tough time.

If in line at the cashier in the supermarket and the person ahead or behind you puts something back because they can't afford it, buy it for them. Do it quietly and without a fuss — your aim is to help the person, not embarrass them.

Donate your old prom dress or tuxedo to an organization which redistributes these to teen boys and girls for their special occasions. And, while we're on the subject, do you really need to hang onto your wedding dress or tuxedo? I have never regretted setting anything free to bless others.

3. Whether you give of your time or your money, whether you do it formally via a charitable organization or off your own bat, be a cheerful giver. Do it with grace, love, and a spirit of generosity, not smug self-satisfaction or begrudging charity.

Give with grace and humility. Your aim is to help, not embarrass, humiliate or make others feel that they now "owe you."

---

4. Don't brag about your good deeds.

If you do something kind, do it quietly. If you post about it on social media, then you're doing it for you — for the praise and attention it brings you. And you're using the person you helped as a prop to make you look good. This is self-aggrandizement, not kindness.

Take a tip from the anonymous donors in the story and give simply because it's the right thing to do.

5. Once you've given, it's not yours to control any longer.

If we give money or things, they become the property of the recipient, and we don't get to say how they should spend or use it. This can be tough, but what we give away is no longer ours to control.

Also, we shouldn't get upset if our beneficiary doesn't seem sufficiently grateful for what we've given. Sometimes people are so shocked or taken aback, that they forget to do the thanking as we would like them to.

Many years ago, I heard a live broadcast on a radio station where a lucky listener won *a house!* And then did not say thank you. I thought she was totally ungrateful, but the show host later told us that she'd called him afterwards and explained that she had been stunned at the time, and literally bereft of speech. Crying, she'd expressed her gratitude fully in her call to him.

The strangers you do kindness for might not know where to find you later. Or their tough lives may have hardened them into tight balls of bitterness and fear, and they may simply not be able to say thank you in the way you would like. They might be suspicious of kindness — in the past, it might have come with strings attached.

You're giving in order to help, not to get thanks or garner recognition.

Your goal is to assist, not to purchase appreciation or praise. Besides, you're not actually giving to that individual or organization, you're giving to the universe, to life itself. Remind yourself that you're not giving because of who *they* are, you're giving because of who *you* are — fortunate, generous and kind-hearted.

Trust that by doing the right thing, you've improved the world.

6. Give back and pay forward.

Has an organization or charity ever helped you or yours? Be like the red kettle donors and give back. I regularly help a local home for girls in need where my mother and aunts spent some time in their very deprived childhoods. It gives me such a kick to think about the love and assistance coming full circle, and spiraling out even wider into the future. Because I just know that some of the girls currently housed there will make great successes of their lives, and will themselves pay it back in the future.

Be like the Doughnut Lassies and pay it forward. Help, even though you don't anticipate getting anything in return. Start something good. Initiate a new ripple of kindness in the world — the world can always do with more!

7. A little is better than nothing.

Don't let the thought that you can't do much lead you to do nothing. Remember the coffee and doughnuts. Do what you can, and trust that the universe will take your tiny offering and expand its reach beyond what you could have anticipated.

THE TAKEAWAY

Be kind.
Be kind whenever, wherever, however, and to whomever you can. Try to be the Johnny Appleseed of kindness, scattering seeds of goodness as you walk through life, planting orchards of giving and helping that will bear fruit far into the future.

CRABS IN A BUCKET

Do other people try to pull you down when you're trying to lift yourself up? Do friends, family or colleagues sabotage your attempts to move on, or improve your life? Perhaps you're a crab in a bucket.

THE STORY

If you've ever been to a fresh fish market, you'll notice that if the sellers have live crabs, they keep them in a shallow bucket or crate, which is left uncovered.

The reason for this is that crabs almost never escape their container. The minute one crab starts climbing up the side of the bucket, the other crabs grab its legs and climb onto its back, pulling it back down again. This process gets repeated with every crab that tries to climb up, with the result that *no* crab escapes.

There are many theories as to why crabs do this — some think they may be trying to protect their fellow crab from drying out in the outside world. Others hypothesize that the other crabs, seeing the first one trying to get away, are also trying to escape, and using the first crab as a sort of ladder or leg-up. It seems to be an instinct for crabs that when they can't swim, they pull on stuff, even on other crabs, in an attempt to move.

All I know for sure is that a crab who tries to escape and reach a place where it would be safe and in its element, never gets a shot at doing it due to the efforts — well or badly intentioned — of its fellows.

123

Even worse, the crabs mutually assure their collective doom — by not letting any escape, they ensure that all will wind up in the cooking pot!

ANALYSIS

Whatever the reason why crabs engage in this self-defeating behavior, they're operating on instinct. What's the excuse for humans? Because people do this to each other all the time.

Crab mentality is a zero-sum way of thinking, summed up by the belief that, "If I can't have it, neither will you." There are plenty of individuals, but also families and groups of people who do everything in their power to destroy or undermine the ambitions of anyone who tries to improve themselves.

Try to rise above and, sure as sugar, someone will try to tear you down.

When you attempt to do something a new and better way, or you're working to escape limiting conditions of living, or to rise above self-defeating thoughts, mostly folks will ignore you. As long as you're not succeeding, you're just a crackpot, a deluded dreamer, a fool who just doesn't understand the way the "real world" works. But when your efforts start to pay dividends, when you stick your head above the rim of the bucket and get a glimpse of the exciting potential beyond, crab-people get nervous and start attacking.

Who?

Crab-people are found everywhere, but it's often those nearest to us who have the most power to impact negatively on our plans.

Most families have beliefs about themselves, and dysfunctional families usually have negative beliefs. (For example: *We just can't hold onto money; we're a family of drinkers, all right; we're not uppity — good-enough is good enough for us; we were born in the ghetto and that's where we'll die; the men in this family are losers.*) Family members may get uncomfortable when one member begins disproving the family rule or belief, but this type of thinking is not limited to families.

Members of work teams might resent those who work harder, or come up with great ideas, or apply for promotions. Many trade unions demand across-the-board increases which de-incentivize individual achievement. Wanting to rise above the work strata you started in may be viewed as being disloyal, or as sucking up to management.

There may be career groups where alternate thinkers are labelled as "maverick" or "dangerous" or unprofessional. The field of medicine, for example, is rife with this. Different specialties deride each other, and traditional allopathic medicine tends to dismiss or mock alternate or complementary approaches.

Often the first individuals to demand change, or to hypothesize a different way of doing things, are the ones who get the worst criticism and most negative reaction. History is full of such examples. Think of poor persecuted Galileo Galilei and Copernicus, who insisted that the earth revolved around the sun, rather than the other way around; and Charles Darwin, who hypothesized that species evolve and was met with derision, dismissal from his professional colleagues, and personal attacks on his character and integrity.

Dr. Ignaz Semmelweis was ignored and belittled for urging his fellow doctors to wash their hands before attending to birthing mothers in obstetric clinics, and was committed to an asylum for his efforts to pioneer antiseptic measures. English welfare campaigner Emily Hobhouse devoted herself to improving the conditions of British concentration camps housing Boer women and children in the second Anglo-Boer War in South Africa, but was met with scathing hostility and criticism when she returned home. American aviatrix Amelia Earhart became the first female pilot to cross the Atlantic despite massive opposition from those who believed that the cockpit was no place for a woman, while Steve Jobs and Steve Wozniak pioneered personal computers, despite being told that there was a worldwide market for only a handful of these.

There are endless groupings — professional, geographical, political, economic, religious, cultural, and even racial — where bucking the established patterns is seen as being disloyal, as a betrayal of your roots, your group affiliation or religion, or "the cause". You may be labeled selfish or a sell-out, and you may be guilt-tripped into falling back into the bucket. Your affiliations are set up as an either-or proposition: *you're either with us, or you're against us. And if you're with us, don't try to change things, don't try to go one better than the rest of us.*

"Just who do you think you are?" they'll demand angrily, as if who you are cannot be better.

How?

The crab-people who feel less than, have many ways to make those who seem set to escape, to grow or succeed, feel less than, too. They might criticize you, shame you or label you — as crazy, a traitor, deluded, etc. These days, of course, they might do this via social media, which amplifies their mean, derogatory messages.

The attack can range from subtly critical comments, all the way through to physical attacks and/or murder — remember Malala Yousafzai? She became Pakistan's leading activist for female education and the youngest-ever Nobel Prize laureate after being shot in the head by a Taliban gunman for attending school and speaking out in support of education for girls.

Crab-people often attack the aspect of you that is winning you success or attention, saying, "You're not as clever as you think you are," or perhaps, "Guys don't like girls who are too clever," to someone who's achieving academically. Or, to someone who is entering the modelling profession, "You're not attractive. I don't know what they see in you!" or "You're so vain." Instantly, the victim is tempted to act stupid, underperform, find ways of looking utterly average, or hide their light under a bushel.

But crab-people can also attack you for something tangential, something not directly related to the aspect of you they envy, because ultimately, their goal is to damage or destroy your self-esteem and confidence.

If you lose faith in yourself, you'll allow yourself to fall right back into the bucket, not believing you have what it takes to make it out there.

Moreover, you'll serve as a warning to others — *Malala took a stand, and look what happened to her. I'd better keep my head down.*

Why?

Human motivations for pulling others down are easier to understand than the mysterious workings of the crustacean mind.

Crab-people usually have a win-lose orientation to life. You've heard the saying, "Misery loves company"? These folks feel inferior and would rather nobody win if they themselves can't.

And for them to feel like winners, others must lose. Unfortunately, when interactions between people, ideologies and nations are dominated by this competitive approach — rather than a cooperative win-win attitude — nobody wins in the long run.

Crabs in the bucket is the ultimate lose-lose scenario.

Crab-people also tend to have a scarcity mentality, rather than a mindset of abundance. They believe that everything — resources, success, opportunities, potential partners, money, freedom — is in short supply, and they're more likely to get a portion of the good stuff if they ensure that you don't.

It's like thinking of the world and its opportunities as a finite pizza pie — *the bigger your slice, the less there is for me.* Except the world doesn't work this way. Opportunities are abundant, probably infinite. There's a reason why we speak of *making* money and *creating* opportunities. There isn't an existing pie of the good stuff. The more we succeed, the more we create, employ, spend, and spread the joy.

Remember how one of the hypotheses for why crabs behave as they do is that they're trying to protect each other? The same is true of humans. Sometimes, crab-people are acting with the best of intentions — they're trying to protect you from failing, getting hurt, making a fool of yourself, losing your shirt on a new venture, or being vulnerable outside the protection of the gang.

"Be careful!" is their constant message. "It's dangerous out there!"

Unfortunately, though their intentions might be kind or honorable, the net effect is the same. You develop a crisis of confidence which prevents you from surmounting your barriers, and you stay trapped in your bucket.

A less obvious reason that motivates crab-people is that the success of one (individual, family or organization) challenges those who don't succeed. They may have told themselves that their failure or stagnation is due to being trapped or constricted by circumstances beyond their control. Partly, of course, it is — when you grow up poor, or without access to resources, or in a group that is discriminated against, it's harder to succeed than when you're born or bred into privilege. But the error is in thinking it's *impossible* to escape. It's an easy belief to adopt, because it lets you off the hook of striving and doing the hard work of lifting yourself out of the bucket.

The success story is uncomfortable, then, because it demonstrates that success *is* in fact possible, and that crab-people may be clinging to excuses, rather than reasons, or that they may have given up and succumbed to helplessness and hopelessness. When you succeed, you're a walking, talking example of what *can* be accomplished, and those who are determined or content to stay in their comfort zones and complain about how unfair the world is, won't like that.

A final reason is that it is certainly easier to tear someone down than to build yourself up, *or* to tackle the structural inequalities of the big issues that oppress you, such as poverty, racism, inferior education systems, ableism, corporate and government corruption, sexism, etc. Crab-people invest their energy in criticizing others rather than coming up with solutions or alternatives.

Critics believe it's easier to level the playing fields by knocking someone down, than by lifting themselves up.

As an aside, I'd like to point out that when crabs start pulling each other down and holding each other back, those who have a vested interest in preserving the status quo are delighted, because now you're fighting with each other, instead of tackling the real source of the problem. In therapy, we say the abuser's work is done when the victim starts abusing themselves. In this broader context, the oppressor's work is done when the oppressed no longer allow each other to rise up and defy their circumstances.

The sad thing is, the crabs in the bucket have everything they need to allow all of them to escape. If they worked together to boost the first crab, and then that one extended a leg to help the next, they could build a ladder-like chain of escape. But, instead of cooperating, they compete. Rather than building up, they tear down. They hinder rather than help. And in the end, they all stay stuck.

Other people may be comfortable with your staying just where, and the way, you are. The question is: are *you?*

Climbing up the walls of your bucket will be hard work, but you can do it. Shake off those who would undermine your confidence.

An old Chinese proverb states: The person who says it cannot be done, should not interrupt the person doing it.

ACTION STEPS

1. What is your bucket?

Put some time and effort into identifying anything that holds you back. What beliefs, living conditions, family attitudes or patterns, structural inequalities, disabilities, or personality traits, keep you stuck?

2. Who are your crabs?

Who holds you back? Who doesn't want you to escape? Remember some of them may be people who love you and care about your welfare, and might believe they are only trying to keep you safe.

Who in your circles (family, friends, colleagues, political affiliates, neighbors, church, etc.) obstructs or undermines you? What messages do they send your way that really hit home and punch holes in your confidence?

3. Decide what you want to do about these crabs and their messages.
   Here are some options:

3.1 Assess

See if there's anything useful that you can glean from what they're saying, then keep that and discard the rest.

People might assert that you can't make a living from being an artist, actor or writer, for example, and insist that you must therefore stay in your nine-to-five job in the conventional job market. This is not completely true, but there is an element of useful advice in it. So, before quitting your day job, perhaps you could save up six months to a year's worth of money to cover your living expenses while you get your new line of work up to speed. Or you could start scaling up your hobby and scaling back your day job until the former is generating more income than the latter.

3.2 Confront

Chat to the person you think is pulling you down or holding you back in a calm and non-accusatory way.

Say something like, *When you tell me it's not possible, or that I'll never succeed, it damages my confidence. I know you've seen a lot of the world and that you're trying to protect me, and I appreciate that. But I'm going to try anyway, even if it means I fail a couple of times along the way, as I probably will. And I'd value your support and encouragement so much more than your cautions.*

3.3 Ignore them.

See their message as being a projection of the way *they* feel, rather than believing it says anything about you. They're talking about themselves, not you. Feel free to shake it off. What would the great minds, leaders and artists of history ever have achieved if they'd crumbled in the face of criticism?

3.4 Start climbing out of your bucket and keep climbing.

Make an action-list today of ten things you'd need to accomplish to take you closer to being free of whatever it is that holds you back from achieving your goals.

Now, break each of those items into smaller action steps, and keep breaking them down until no step will take longer than thirty minutes to accomplish.

Every day, highlight two of these small tasks, and do them.

> *Viewed as a whole, change can look overwhelmingly difficult, and can leave you demotivated.*
> *When you break the process down into bite-sized chunks, it becomes so much easier to imagine and to achieve.*

4. Quit acting like a crab.

Do you yourself sometimes behave like a crab person? If so, cut that foolishness out right now. You can't lift yourself up by pulling someone else down. You can't fill yourself by emptying another. You can't improve your life by limiting someone else's. Life is not a zero-sum game — someone else's gain is not your loss.

Instead, support trailblazers. Celebrate their success. They are making a path that will be easier for you to follow. They are creating a success story which can inspire you. Ask them to mentor you, and model yourself after them.

> *Instead of saying, "If I can't have it, neither can he," say, "If he can do it, so can I!"*

Go a step further and pay it forward by giving that person a supportive leg up.

5. If you're the crab that escaped, pay it back.

Reach back down and give someone else a hand up. If you're already out of the bucket, throw back a lifeline and try to assist those who are still stuck. (Just don't let them pull you back in!) Become a mentor and a guide; share what you've learned, and help when you can.

6. Replace your scarcity mindset with a belief in abundance.

A scarcity mindset is especially common to those who grew up in impoverished circumstances — that's how it was for you back then. But it's not how it has to be now or in the future. You can choose to believe differently.

Craft an affirmation for yourself that addresses your bucket restrictions.

If, for example, your lack of confidence holds you back, tell yourself:
I am a strong, confident person. I can do this!

If your issue relates to escaping a family tradition of failure, tell yourself:
I am strong, talented and successful. Every day my life gets better and better.

As with all affirmations, make sure yours is phrased in the first person ("*I* am strong"), present tense ("I *am* strong," not "I will be strong") and in the positive ("I am *strong*," not "I am not weak"). Repeat your new truth to yourself seventy-five times a day, even if you don't believe it — *especially* when you don't believe it. One day in the not too distant future, you'll realize it's becoming your new reality!

THE TAKEAWAY

Crabs don't belong in buckets. It's not their natural habitat; it's not where they thrive.

The same is true for you. There's no merit in staying trapped in poverty, ignorance, prejudice, pessimism, or whatever it is that holds you and yours back.

Isn't it time you climbed all the way out of your bucket?

THE MAGIC QUESTION

Do you have a dream for your life — personal or professional? Do you have a big goal that you'd like to achieve, but there seem to be too many obstacles in the way? Are you faced with a big decision and battling to decide which way to go? Here is a story that might help.

THE STORY

Our first child, a son, was born perfectly healthy after a problem-free pregnancy. But the birth itself was a nightmare — protracted, painful, scary, and it ended in an emergency caesarean section.

I came out of the hospital three days later feeling like I'd gone ten rounds with a heavy-weight boxer. I was bruised, sore, emotionally traumatized, and utterly exhausted. And now I had a tiny, helpless baby to take care of.

Those first few months were hard, especially since most of my family and friends lived in far-off corners of the world, and I had very limited support. I loved my baby, but there were aspects of mothering I found difficult — subsuming my identity as an individual and career woman into being a mother, spending most of my time nursing and caring for my infant, and losing the freedom to come and go as I pleased. It wasn't easy, but I could cope with these aspects.

A female colleague at work who'd recently had her first baby got me through the early days by telling me, "The first week is the worst. It gets better after that, promise!" "Just get to three weeks, you can't

135

believe how much better you'll feel then!" "Hang in there, at six weeks he'll start smiling and everything gets easier!" "Just wait until he can eat solids and sit up, then it will be smooth sailing."

Well, twenty-two years later, I can confirm that parenting is never "smooth sailing." It did get much easier, however, and even in those early months when I felt overwhelmed, incompetent, and way out of my depth, I could see small improvements. I could believe that there would come a time when I would (more or less) know what I was doing, and when my baby wouldn't need me every minute of the day.

But there was one aspect which did not get better. My baby simply didn't sleep — not like other babies, not like the baby books said he should, not like I'd expected. He didn't nap in the day and didn't sleep through the night. At first, he would sleep only about fifty minutes at one go, before coming fully awake and alert (unlike his mother.) Over time, that lengthened to two hour stretches, and eventually the odd three-hour stretch. When he woke, I'd have to change him, feed him, change him again, and then try to get him back to sleep, before the whole process started all over again. This went on for three years. Three. Years.

Over the course of three years, he slept through the night on fewer than five occasions.

Now the thing is, I *love* sleep. I'm a talented sleeper. I can fall asleep in seconds and sleep deeply. I can sleep ten hours at a stretch. If there were an Olympic event for sleeping, I'd be a gold medal contender.

I *need* at least eight hours a night, every night, to deal with the challenges of daily life. I'm better on nine hours, and deliriously happy on ten. So not having my sleep was a serious blow to me. I felt light-headed and dizzy with lack of sleep, nauseated, exhausted, fuzzy-minded. I'm not exaggerating when I say it felt potentially fatal — there were days when I thought that I might die from lack of sleep. It scares me now to think that I was working, studying for my Master's degree, and driving while chronically sleep-deprived. I don't know how I did it.

Eventually, of course, my son did start sleeping through the night, and now he, too, is a sleep champion of note. And oh, how delicious, how restorative and precious it was when I started getting a full night's sleep once again.

By then, I had graduated and was practicing as a psychologist. My son was a happy, healthy three-and-a-half-year-old — weaned, walking, talking, potty-trained, attending play-school and, of course, sleeping. The parental heavy-lifting of the infant and toddler years was behind me. He was intelligent, cute and funny — I adored him.

It was time for my husband and me to decide if we wanted another baby. I come from a large family and I'd always wanted at least two children, but the thought of another birth (potentially as horrible as the first), all those difficult early days (and now with another child to care for), combining it all with a career (we couldn't afford for me to be a stay-at-home-mom), and — most especially — of going back to broken nights? It filled my heart with trepidation and doubt.

I booked an appointment with a psychologist colleague to discuss the issue and get help making a decision. She listened to me talk about labor, changing diapers, being glued to a baby's side for months, losing freedom due to breastfeeding (I loved nursing, but not the lack of freedom that went with it), and most especially to my complaints about lack of sleep.

Then she said, "It seems like all the concerns you have are about things that happen in the early years; they don't last forever."

I nodded. This was true.

Then she asked the magic question, "In five years' time, what will you wish you had done now?"

I reeled from the power of that question. Then I smiled, thanked her, told her the session was over, shook her hand and left. I had my answer.

Of course, I wanted another baby. In five years' time, if I went that route, I'd have a little child who was also walking, talking, weaned and sleeping through the night. He or she would be older, and therefore (for me) easier to parent.

I'd been so focused on the challenges and hassles of the short-term that I'd nearly made a decision which I would bitterly have regretted in the long term.

Postscript: Just under a year later, I gave birth to a healthy and beautiful baby girl. The birth was better and, the second time around, I did feel more competent as a mother. That's what mothers mean when they say it's easier the second time around. There isn't less to do — there's *more* — but you feel better able to cope because you've done it before and know it's doable, plus you've picked up a ton of tricks to make things easier.

However, just as with my son, my daughter only started sleeping through the night at around the age of three years. And she, too, turned out to be a champion sleeper in the long run.

ANALYSIS

Sometimes, when we're facing a challenging task or a difficult decision, the effort involved can seem monumental and the obstacles insurmountable. Often, we give up too quickly — daunted by the hardship we anticipate in the short-term.

Keep your eye on the long-term goal, think about how much better things will be if you push through the next few months or years.

How sad I would have been if I'd forgone the opportunity to know and love this second magnificent, talented, loving child for the sake of three years of unbroken sleep. It would have been the stupidest decision of my life.

In five years' time, you're going to be five years older anyway. Would you rather be that age and have earned your degree, emigrated to the new country to take up the fabulous opportunity there, be the published author of a book, or the owner of a new business? Or would you rather have only exactly what you already have now?

Now, there's nothing special about the period of five years. Your question could be, "In one year's time, what will I wish I had done now?" or even, "Next week, what will I wish I had done this week?" The point is that you initiate and complete action in the *now* to accomplish what you would like to have in the *future*.

It's the difference between living a proactive, goal-directed life and a reactive, haphazard, hit-and-miss life.

Your desired future destination determines your necessary course of action in the present.

ACTION STEPS

1. What's your *BHAG*?

What's your Big Hairy Audacious Goal? What's something daunting and impressive you want to achieve? What's something you're already considering, but the journey to get there just seems too difficult? It may be something like studying for a qualification, going through couple's therapy to improve your relationship with your partner, learning a new language, building a house, planting a garden from scratch, founding some charitable organization, starting a business, having or adopting a child, or something else you seriously want in your life.

What action or achievement will most make you feel like you've accomplished a cherished dream?

Write it down.

2. Figure out the time line.

Calculate how old you'll be when you accomplish it, if you start now.

Calculate how old you'll be if you *don't* start it now.

Which would you rather be, or have, in your future?

3. One step at a time

Break your task or challenge down into smaller tasks, and then smaller steps, and even smaller ones. You'll find that it looks much less daunting when written up this way. Every journey begins with a single step, and then another, and another.

By the yard, life is hard. By the inch, life's a cinch.

---

4. Use telescopic and microscopic vision.

To get through hectically difficult times, cultivate telescopic and microscopic vision, and ditch the binoculars of the middle-distance view for now.

Let me explain what I mean. Telescopes are what we use to look into the far distance. With your imaginary telescope, train your gaze on your long-term dream. Imagine how fabulous it will feel many months or years from now to have the difficulties of this intermediate period behind you, to have accomplished what you set out to do. Remind yourself of all the positive consequences that will flow from achieving your goal. Visualize how proud you will feel of yourself. This dream will motivate you to begin, as well as to follow through. Repeat this exercise from time to time to remind yourself *why* you've undertaken your journey.

Microscopic view means you focus on what you need to *do* today, this morning, right this minute! What action can you start or complete *now* that takes you a step closer to your ultimate goal? This will get you moving and help build momentum. We can dream about the future, but we can only live and act in the present.

Action happens in the present.
Action in the present brings about the future.

Binoculars are what we use to see the finer details on things in the middle distance. If you're struggling to get through a hard patch, these can easily cause you to feel overwhelmed. If you know every last detail of exactly how hard your task will be, chances are, you won't even begin. Looking into the next few months can be daunting and demotivating. If today is so hard, you ask yourself, how will I possibly be able to cope with several months or even years of this?

You'll be able to cope by keeping your gaze both on the long-term vision, and on the immediate tasks and challenges of today. Put down those imaginary binoculars — they're only scaring and demotivating you.

THE TAKEAWAY

Remember the magic question: In the future, what will you wish you had done today?

BABOONS AND PUMPKINS

What are you too attached to? What can't you let go of? What are the risks of keeping yourself stuck? Read on to discover if you're a baboon!

THE STORY

Wherever in the world monkeys or baboons and humans co-exist in close proximity, there will be conflict. The primates are clever creatures, not easily scared off and are quite capable (as I've seen first-hand here in Africa) of trashing cars, houses, vegetable patches, crops, and orchards in their inventive quest for food.

So, it's not surprising that wherever people are bothered by these "nuisance" animals — in Africa, South East Asia, or on various tropical islands — there's a version of this story. I don't know how many are true, but I've seen videos which convince me that the so-called monkey-trap works at least some of the time. And anyway, it's a great parable.

Here in South Africa, the story involves baboons and pumpkins. In other parts of the world, the trap uses tethered coconuts and rice, or gourds and nuts, or bottles and sweets — whatever your bait, the principle of the trap remains the same.

The farmer whose crops and food gardens are being regularly raided by wandering troops of foraging baboons selects one of the largest pumpkins in his vegetable patch. Into the top of it, he carves a small hole — just large enough for a baboon to push its hand through. The farmer might slip a banana inside, or just trust in the tempting appeal of the fresh seeds nesting in the juicy pulp inside the pumpkin. Then he walks away and takes up a position in a nearby vantage spot, where he waits, rifle in his hands.

When the troop passes through, one baboon will inevitably investigate the pumpkin and stick its hand through the hole to get to the juicy treat inside. But with its paw now clenched in a fist around the seeds or the banana, it's too big to be pulled back out through the hole.

The baboon fusses, thrashes around, and yanks and pulls with all its might, but it doesn't (initially at least) think to unclench its hand and let go of the seeds. The large pumpkin is too heavy for the baboon to carry off, so it stays — trapped by its own stubborn determination not to give up its prize.

Eventually the baboon lets go — probably more in frustration and exhaustion than as a planned strategy to free itself — but if the farmer (or monkey-hunter in other parts of the world) is quick enough to get there while the creature is still hanging on, it's bad news for that animal.

ANALYSIS

A person watching the struggling, trapped baboon might wonder, "Why doesn't it just let go? Stupid creature!"

But we humans are often no smarter. We too are snared by the bait of things that appeal to us.

We are trapped by our refusal to let go of what we think we must have.

What are some of the things that people hang onto, to their own detriment?

Sometimes we are trapped by our possessions, stuck in a rising pile of material goods. Our desire for these things often gets us into trouble

— we live beyond our means, accumulate debt, and are trapped in the rat-race to pay for them. We can be trapped in jobs we loathe by the golden handcuffs of good money.

Many people are trapped by their absolute and overriding need for approval. It keeps them obsessed with appearance; it leads them to putting up with substandard treatment, to living within the limiting boundaries drawn by others. They live to please others, and ignore or neglect their own needs.

Sometimes, what we grasp onto is a short-term reward — as delicious as the treat to the monkey — of something as simple as a decadent piece of cake (when we're trying to lose weight); a shopping spree (when we're trying to save money); a snort of cocaine (when we know the danger of addiction); a one-night stand with a sexy someone (risking our long-term relationship).

One by one, our impulsive behaviors stack up, keeping us trapped in the long-term wasteland of addiction, obesity, financial problems, crippled relations and broken families. We are held prisoner by the childish attitude of, "But I waaaaant it!"

In gambling, the excitement and thrill of that next bet and the uncertain hope of possibly winning keeps you trapped in addiction. And gambling doesn't just happen in casinos. We gamble with our lives when we have unprotected sex. We gamble with our physical and mental health when we take "recreational" drugs. Sometimes, we make a mistake and screw up — that happens to every single one of us — but when we repeatedly make the same mistake, hoping for the high-stakes but nigh-impossible payout, then we are gambling, and addicted to the biological highs of adrenalin and dopamine secretions.

Sometimes, we hang onto things, people and situations which don't look appealing at first sight, but which offer the rewards that come with staying in our comfort zones — even when they are painful or dangerous places. These rewards include such things as stability, predictability, the strange pleasure of being a martyred victim, being excused from the hard work of change, attention from others for our problem, etc. These "secondary gains" keep us trapped in the not-so-comfortable comfort zone of dysfunction.

For example, negative thoughts and ways of perceiving the world, and endlessly ruminating about the past or bad elements of the present, can help keep you trapped in depression. Holding onto grudges and resentment keeps you trapped in the grim misery of self-righteousness. Holding onto your excess weight excuses you from getting out there into the dating scene, where lies the risk and potential pain of rejection and heartache.

Life is full of snares for the unwary. Status; power or popularity; the desire to be in control of everything; the need to be right or to win every argument; fashion, security, resentment, regrets, grief, anxiety, blame, prejudices, a sense of entitlement, shame, bitterness, pessimism, anger — there is a certain pleasure in clinging to each of these things.

If the trapped baboon could talk, what would it be screeching? Humans stuck in this kind of trap often blame everything but themselves. They blame the person who set the trap; they blame God or fate or destiny for the smallness of the hole; they blame the pumpkin for being in their path. They blame the government, or their childhood.

When we blame others, it leaves us powerless to improve things, to get ourselves free, because how do you change others, or the government, let alone destiny or God?

And if those pumpkin seeds could talk, what would they say to the baboon? *Hold on tight, never let go, I am what you want!*

What do our traps say to us? I think they try to convince us that *this* is what we really want, and if we just hold on for long enough, we'll get to enjoy it.

But this *isn't* what we really want. What we really want is what we'll *feel* when we have what we think we want. That's complicated! Let's go through it slowly.

What you really want,
*is what you'll **feel**,*
when you have
what you think you want.

So, we think we want money, but what we really want is to feel *safe* or protected against the unpredictable challenges of the future. Or we think we want power, when what we really crave is *respect*. We think we want the short-term burst of pleasure that comes with consuming, but what will really fill us is a long-term sense of *contentment*. We think we want the escape of the high, but what we desire in our core is its opposite — a sense of *meaning* and purpose.

In fact, hanging onto our pumpkin seeds (whatever form they take in our lives) usually keeps us trapped in the opposite of what we truly need and deeply desire. *Letting go* (not holding on) is what sets us free and impels us on the path of seeking and bringing about what we truly desire.

Monkeys are ignorant of the mechanics of the trap, and they are creatures of instinct. But we humans? We stupidly and *willfully* cling to the very things that imprison us.

Who's the dumb baboon now?

ACTION STEPS

1. Prevention is better than cure.

Be like a wise old baboon who learns from the mistakes of others, or its own past. Try to spot the trap and not take the bait in the first place!

2. Identify what it is that you're holding onto.

What's keeping you from freedom? What — if you just surrendered it — would set you free to live a healthier, happier life? What issues, regrets, beliefs, habits or behaviors are taking away from your freedom? What pumpkin seeds do you need to let go of in order to set yourself free?

3. Identify the cost.

The trapped baboon will lose its life. The trapped monkey will be sold into captivity. What does it cost *you* to stay stuck? If your life continues along this current trajectory, where will you wind up?

4. Dare to believe that letting go and moving on is possible.

If you've been trapped for a long time, it may seem inconceivable to you that you could ever get free again. Start with the faith that it is possible to let go.

5. Let go and get out of there.

Replace your "pumpkin seeds" with different, healthier beliefs, habits and behaviors in the world beyond the pumpkin so you don't feel quite so empty-handed once you've let go.

Here are some examples:

Money: Instead of spending that $20 on something you don't need, put it in a savings account, or stick it in your credit card account. Watching your increasing financial nest-egg, or your decreasing debt will give you a dopamine buzz just as surely as the short-term pleasure of a new purchase, plus it will leave you in a safer place financially.

Romance: Instead of flirting with the danger of an affair, take action to deepen the romance of your relationship with your partner — go away for a romantic weekend; plan a candlelit picnic in the backyard one evening; get a book on improving your relationship or putting some pep into your sex life and *actually do the exercises*; do something fun like meeting in a hotel bar as if you were strangers and flirting with each other, or get professional help — it's cheaper than a divorce!

Eating: Instead of treating yourself with the piece of cake, how about you treat yourself with a bowl of delicious fresh raspberries, or a bottle of marinated artichokes from the deli, or something non-edible — a new magazine (but not a beauty or fashion magazine, which will only make you feel fat, ugly and old!), an afternoon nap, or a bunch of beautiful flowers.

Negativity: Instead of noticing and hanging onto negative interpretations of your life, practice gratitude. Search for the lesson or the silver lining in everything that happens. Make this your new habit.

6. Getting help is smart, not weak.

If you need professional assistance to help get out of your trap — get it! Seeking help isn't an admission of weakness. It's a sign of intelligence and a commitment to health.

You wouldn't feel "weak" for taking your car to a mechanic if there was smoke coming out from under the hood, would you? You wouldn't feel weak for taking your dog to the vet if it was sick, or your computer to the repair shop if it had a bug, so why feel less-than for seeking out expert assistance for your health, psychological well-being, finances or relationships?

THE TAKEAWAY

Don't be a baboon.
Stop clinging to what keeps you stuck.
Let go and set yourself free.

SPLINTERS — THE GIFT OF PAIN

Would you keep walking on a foot that had a splinter? Do you ignore your non-physical injuries? It's time to learn the gift of pain.

THE STORY

Imagine you're going for a walk, and every time you step down on one foot, you feel a sharp pain. What would you do?

You'd probably sit down and examine your foot to try find the source of discomfort. If you saw a splinter or a thorn sticking out of your flesh, you'd carefully remove it, perhaps apply some antiseptic ointment, and stick a Band-Aid over the little wound, and then keep walking, confident that it would heal.

It you didn't attend to it immediately, each step would push the splinter in deeper, until removing it would require a more serious and painful procedure, involving cutting it out and upping the risk of infection. Recovery from this would be slower; it might require expensive medical intervention, and in the meantime, it would still hurt on every step.

If you didn't remove it at all, you would risk getting a festering wound which could poison your whole foot. Sometimes the body encapsulates the foreign body in a mass of protective tissue which may become inflamed or infected, causing complications to the surrounding tissue and possibly even to bone. If the foreign body is a spine from a plant or animal, the result can be toxic to the patient.

People who suffer with leprosy must do daily checks of their body, because they have lost sensation in parts of it. Not feeling the pain of cuts or splinters, the individual may leave these untreated and infection or even gangrene can set in, resulting in the amputation of a limb or life-threatening sepsis.

ANALYSIS

Pain is unpleasant, but it's not all bad.

Pain can sometimes be a gift. It draws our attention to the fact that something is wrong, injured, out of alignment, or infected. It reminds us to treat our wounds so that they can heal and we can be healthy.

This is true of emotional and psychological pain, too. When you ignore it, it doesn't go away. It still hurts. It sucks up a lot of your time and energy to try ignore it, repress it, make yourself numb, or distract yourself from it. By not dealing with it, there's a very real risk that it can wind up spreading, contaminating other parts of yourself and your life, and poisoning your emotional well-being, your relationships and your all-round functioning.

As is the case with the splinter, it's so much easier to deal with psychological wounds when they're small and fresh.

ACTION STEPS

1. Make a list of the emotional "wounds" you have suffered in your life. Commit to dealing with them, and to starting that process today.

2. Get professional help if need be, or talk to a trusted friend, family member, or community or religious leader. Join a support group of people who are dealing with the same issue — in person or online.

3. Research your issue and find out what you can do to help remove this "splinter" and prevent any further infection.

4. Pay attention to what — and who — hurts you. This is often a good indication that this behavior, place, person or attitude is not health-promoting.

THE TAKEAWAY

If you're hurting, take the time to stop, identify the source of the pain, assess the damage, and deal with it properly.
You wouldn't neglect physical wounds, so don't leave life wounds to fester, either.

A Jar of Stones and Sand

Are you living your life with the end in mind? Or are you perpetually "busy" in a way that doesn't ultimately enrich your life? Take a few minutes to digest the layers of this story.

The Story

This is a popular tale and there are many versions of it, but I'll go with the one that credits a wise old professor of philosophy with the wisdom of the lesson.

One fine morning, a professor stands in front of his class of students, and says, "I know how busy your lives are, how tightly packed your schedules are, but I hope you will grant me a few minutes for a demonstration, because I have a critically important lesson to impart to you."

Eager, the students grab their pens and paper to capture the lecture's main points.

But instead of switching on a projector or writing on the board, the professor places a large, glass mason jar on the desk in front of him. Into this he carefully places several fist-sized rocks, until the jar is filled and no more rocks will fit inside.

Then he turns to the class of students, who are mystified as to what he is doing, and asks, "Is this vase full?"

They all nod and agree. "Yes, it's full."

"Really?" the professor asks.

He brings out a bucket from under his desk, and from it dumps a pile of small pebbles into the jar, shaking it this way and that so that the pebbles fall into the spaces between the larger rocks.

"Is the vase full now?" he asks his students.

"Probably not," they reply, chuckling.

"Correct!" says the professor, hauling out another bucket.

This time he tips sand into the jar, again shaking things around so that the sand trickles into every available space.

"Now is it full?"

"No," the students say.

"Indeed, it is not," he agrees, and pours water from a jug into the jar, filling it full to the brim.

"And what, my dear students, is the moral of this story? What is the point of this demonstration?"

One eager student volunteers, "The point is to show us that no matter how busy you are, no matter how full your schedule is, you can always fit more things in."

"No," says the professor. "The moral is that if you don't put the big things in first, they probably will not fit in later, and may never fit in at all."

To demonstrate, the professor empties the jar and fills it again, but this time he sweeps all the sand in first, then adds the pebbles in a layer on top of that, and finally stacks the rocks on top. And this time, as predicted, all the rocks cannot fit inside the jar.

ANALYSIS

The rocks represent what you truly value. These are the things that will still matter at the end of your life. In fact, they are probably the *only* things that will matter then. For most people, the most important things are your family, your health, your faith, the satisfaction of having led a good life and fulfilled your hopes and dreams, and hopefully even left some kind of a legacy behind you when you go.

If you lost everything else in your life, but the rocks remained, your life would still be meaningful. If you lost even one rock and had all the sand and pebbles you could want, it would not help or matter.

The pebbles are other important things in your life that add meaning — relationships with friends, your work, and your treasured hobbies. It might include satisfying things like travel and study.

The sand and water of your life are those small, trivial things that don't add value to your life, won't matter in the future, and yet consume time, energy and attention in the present.

This includes things like spending time playing games on your phone or watching silly videos on YouTube, watching mindless television or getting caught up in the latest social media storm, trying to keep the house perfectly clean, or running errands. They are distractions and/or time-sucks. Yes, we must do some of these, but when we *prioritize* them — which is what we are doing when we do them first, before we do the important stuff — we run the risk of not having enough time or energy left to pursue what truly matters.

What you do first, and most, is what you are prioritizing.

ACTION STEPS

1. Make a list of your rocks.

What are the most important things in your life? Here are some questions to stimulate your thinking:

Consider things such as health, relationships with your partner and children.

On your death bed, what and who will you wish you'd spent more time with and energy on?

Is there someone you'd like to mentor or sponsor, a life you could help grow?

Is there a cause that you care deeply about that needs championing or support?

Are there still issues in your psychological life that need healing?

What legacy will you leave behind you when you pass? Have you planted a forest, written a book, sponsored the digging of a well in an arid country, taught someone to read, mentored a person who needs encouragement and guidance, contributed of yourself (not just your money) to a cause that matters, built a house or a bridge, or invested in a happy, solid marriage?

Will you be leaving children with great self-esteem, children who know they are loved and important enough to spend time with and get your full attention?

2. Make a list of your pebbles.

What is important and needs to be done, but won't really matter at the end of your life?

3. Make a list of your sand.

What trivialities of life, that won't matter in a week's time, let alone at the end of your life, do you sometimes or regularly fill your days with?

4. Calculate the cost.

Estimate how much time in your average day, week and year you are dedicating to these rocks, pebbles and sand.

Most people who complete this exercise are horrified to discover that they invest time, energy and attention in inverse proportion to the importance of the pursuit. In other words, they spend most of their time and energy, and focus most of their attention, on trivial, unimportant issues, often getting quite worked up and stressed by the most irrelevant things. And they realize how little of their lives centers around the things that truly matter.

For example, how much time have you spent watching TV or hanging out on social media in this last week? And how much dedicated time have you spent with your children, partner or a beloved family member?

On their deathbed, nobody wishes they'd spent more time at the office, or liking posts on Facebook!

---

5. Schedule time for your rocks.

Grab your planner and block off time to spend with your children — playing a game together, spectating at their sport or recital, going for a meal together, or just hanging out and chatting. Switch off your phones and the TV during this time. Focus on each other.

Make a date to spend time with your spouse or partner — have a picnic in the park, or in your back yard, go for a walk together (a gently-paced one, the sort where you have enough breath to speak), or write a long love letter. Go out to dinner and a show, or have a candlelit dinner at home after the children are asleep. Go out to an art gallery or a ballgame. Do something special on your anniversary.

Pay attention to your faith. We are all spiritual beings, as much as we are physical, mental and emotional beings. Whether you restore your spirit in a church, mosque or temple, or in the grand cathedral of nature, spend time and energy on the stuff of the spirit. Pray, meditate, visualize, and/or practice gratitude. Stop and notice beauty and kindness. Celebrate life, and mourn death.

Challenge yourself to think deep thoughts. Grapple with your beliefs and aim for expansion, not exclusion.

Dedicate time — actually block it off in your planner — to devote to creating the type of legacy you'd like to leave behind. How is the world a better place because you lived? Identify what you'd like to accomplish and start doing it. Note that this type of work or creation is vitally important, yet seldom urgent. An entire life can slip by without you lifting a finger to create the legacy you'd like to leave behind. But it's all too easy to leave behind a different legacy — one of passivity, inaction and neglect.

Invest time and energy in sorting out your relationship with *yourself*. Grow your self-esteem, finish your unfinished business with others, forgive or apologize where necessary, and let go of that old baggage you've been lugging around all these years. Confront your demons, tackle your bad habits and addictions.

Your longest relationship in your life will be with yourself — do everything you can to make sure you like, love, and respect yourself.

Book time to exercise this week (and every week), and to prepare healthy food for yourself. Eat at a table, away from phones and TV. Eat the food slowly and mindfully; taste and enjoy it. Be grateful.

6. Set limits on your sand.

Maybe you limit yourself to checking social media once a day for fifteen minutes, or perhaps you could challenge yourself to have a social media "fast" for a month. Try recording only those TV programs you really want to see, and then watch them at a convenient time, after you've attended to some important rocks. That way at least you cut out the advertisements and programs you're just too lazy to switch off.

7. Do the important stuff first.

Most people are at their most energetic and efficient in the morning. Don't start your day with sand (emails, surfing the net, TV, cleaning dust bunnies out from under the sofa). Start it with rocks — do something that matters, that takes you a definite step closer to the life goals you want to achieve and the priorities you want to focus on. You will never *find* the time to do this. You need to *create* time — carve it out, protect it fiercely, schedule it in your planner.

Don't give what really matters only the leftovers of time, energy and attention.

---

8. Track your important work.

Keep a log of the amount of time you spend in your important pursuits, and record the milestones you achieve. In my work as a writer, for example, the most important thing is creating new books, so I keep track of my writing sessions and my word counts. This holds me accountable to my goals.

9. Don't confuse motion with progress.

At regular intervals in your day and week, stop and ask yourself — am I doing something important, or am I just keeping "busy"? Redirect your focus and efforts to the important stuff.

THE TAKEAWAY

If you attend to the big issues first, the small stuff will fall into place. The reverse is not true.
Prioritize the most important aspects of your life.

A FREEZING SNEEZE

How well do you take care of yourself? How's that working for you?

THE STORY

Many years ago, while I was driving on the highway, the driver in the car behind me was so busy chatting to his passenger that he failed to notice how the traffic ahead was backing up. He slammed into the back of my stationary car, sending me into the tow bar of the car in front of me. My car was crunched at both ends, and my back and neck were not happy. But, hey, I could carry on with my busy life, as long as I ignored the ongoing and increasing discomfort. Until one day, I couldn't ignore it anymore.

I was rushing to get dressed for work one cold winter's morning, and as I bent over to fasten my shoes, I sneezed. Immediately, I could tell something had gone wrong. My back muscles had seized — presumably to prevent a disc from slipping — and I was stuck in that bent-double position.

I tried moving slowly, going sideways, stretching gently. Surely this was just a cramp that would soon pass? But every time I moved the slightest bit, every time I even inhaled a breath, there was a viciously sharp pain, which locked me into my paralyzed position. Eventually, I realized I needed assistance.

"Help!" I yelled. "Someone help!"

My bedroom door was closed, and it took a long, agonizing while for anyone to hear my cries above the hubbub of the household's morning rush.

Eventually my mother discovered me, still bent with my nose close to the floor. She called my father and we had a pow-wow about what to do. It was clear I wouldn't be making it to work, but I couldn't even make it to the bed. I literally could not move an inch.

Finally, my father lifted all five-foot-nine-and-a-half of me up, and with my mother's help, hoisted me — still crooked in a C shape — over to my bed. He was as gentle as he could be, but it still hurt like the dickens, and I'm sure my muscles locked into an even deeper spasm as I tensed against the pain.

The doctor was called for a house-visit, and gave me a monster shot of muscle-relaxants and painkillers in the butt. I had to lie in bed for days, and then follow a regime of exercise and physiotherapy which helped, but never entirely fixed the problem.

I have never again sneezed while bending over.

ANALYSIS

The moral of this story amounts to this: don't sneeze (or cough) while bending over, unless you want your back to lock into a spasm.

What? You expected a deeper lesson? Even Freud said, "Sometimes a cigar is just a cigar."

I will add this, if I'd taken better care of myself when my back was first injured, I may have spared myself countless problems and pain down the line. And if I'd *slowed down* a little, listening to the itchy-nosed signal my body sent me, and then stood erect or sat down before sneezing, things would also have played out much better.

ACTION STEPS

1. Take care of yourself.

You will only ever have one body, and it's got to last you all your life. Putting some time, money and effort into self-care isn't selfish, or self-indulgent. It's a responsible investment in your present and your future.

2. Listen when your body whispers; don't make it shout.

I'm not saying that you should grind to a standstill for every minor ache or pain, but if a condition is worsening, there's pain that's not going away, or if something about the way your body works has changed significantly, get it checked.

3. Move your body.

Exercise doesn't have to happen at an expensive gym, and it doesn't have to be for forty minutes, five times a week.

Just get moving. Dance, walk around the block, play a game of soccer with your children, skip in the driveway, take the stairs whenever possible, find an activity you enjoy, and begin blessing your body with movement.

4. Go for regular checkups — medical and dental.

Which ones do you need to schedule *today*?

5. Check yourself regularly.

Do important self-examinations (such as checking for lumps in your breasts or testicles, keeping a watchful eye on moles and pigment marks on your skin). Make this easy to remember by doing it on a regular day, such as the first or last day of every month. A good day for pre-menopausal women to do breast exams, for example, would be on the first day after their period ends, every month. Time your annual checkups around your birthday so you don't forget.

6. Eat well.

Eat as low down on the processing chain as you can. Eat foods that look like themselves (for example, a carrot looks like carrot, but carrot cake looks like cake). Sometimes healthier food options are more expensive than fast foods, but bear in mind that you'll be saving on medical bills and diet plans down the line.

Slow is smooth, and smooth is fast.

---

7. Slow down.

A few more minutes in your daily commute, with your paying absolute attention, rather than rushing and taking chances, could save your life — and other people's, too.

The goal of life is not to live it in a flash.

Sometimes, the slower you go, the quicker you get where you're going. As the Navy SEALs are fond of saying: *slow is smooth, and smooth is fast.*

THE TAKEAWAY

Take care of yourself — you're worth it!

LAST WORD

Take care of yourself - that's pretty much what I've been saying in every story throughout this book. Take care of yourself — body, mind, heart and soul.

In my twenty years of being a psychologist, I've come to believe that therapy works best for those who need it least — for people who are willing, and able, to learn what they need to know and apply it in their lives. For people like you!

Please read and reread all the stories in this book. Do the exercises. Learn and apply the lessons.

My sincere wish is that you take the morals and messages of these stories to heart and that you begin — today! — living a healthier, happier and more successful life.

Gentle Reader,

I hope you enjoyed this book and found it useful. If you did, please consider leaving a short review on your favorite online site to help other readers discover it.

I plan to write more books in the Self-Help Stories series. This first book is general in nature, but the rest will be related to specific themes or topics. If you would like to be notified of new releases in this series, please sign up on my VIP Readers' Group page at my website: www.joannemacgregor.com.

Wishing you a long, happy, healthy life filled with love, laughter and meaning,

- Joanne Macgregor

(Counseling Psychologist)

45591515R00102

Made in the USA
Columbia, SC
22 December 2018